BASKETBALL ANATOMY

Brian Cole, MD
NBA Team Physician of the Year

Rob Panariello, CSCS
USA Strength and Conditioning Hall of Fame

Human Kinetics

Library of Congress Cataloging-in-Publication Data

Library of Congress Cataloging-in-Publication Data
Cole, Brian J.
  Basketball anatomy / Brian Cole, NBA Team Physician of the Year; Rob Panariello.
    pages cm
  Includes bibliographical references.
1. Basketball--Training. 2. Basketball--Physiological aspects. 3. Basketball injuries. 4. Physical
education and training. 5. Physical fitness. I. Panariello, Rob. II. Title.
  GV885.35.C6 2015
  796.323--dc23

                                        2015016189

ISBN: 978-1-4504-9644-5 (print)

Acquisitions Editor: Justin Klug; **Developmental Editor:** Cynthia McEntire; **Associate Managing
Editor:** Nicole Moore; **Copyeditor:** Jan Feeney; **Graphic Designer:** Fred Starbird; **Graphic Artist:**
Tara Welsch; **Cover Designer:** Keith Blomberg; **Photographer (for cover and interior illustra-
tion references):** Neil Bernstein; **Art Manager:** Kelly Hendren; **Associate Art Manager:** Alan L.
Wilborn; **Illustrations:** Jennifer Gibas and Lachina Publishing Services, Inc.; **Printer:** Versa Press

Human Kinetics books are available at special discounts for bulk purchase. Special editions or
book excerpts can also be created to specification. For details, contact the Special Sales Manager
at Human Kinetics.

Printed in the United States of America   10   9   8   7   6   5   4   3   2   1

The paper in this book is certified under a sustainable forestry program.

Human Kinetics
Website: www.HumanKinetics.com

United States: Human Kinetics
P.O. Box 5076
Champaign, IL 61825-5076
800-747-4457
e-mail: humank@hkusa.com

Canada: Human Kinetics
475 Devonshire Road Unit 100
Windsor, ON N8Y 2L5
800-465-7301 (in Canada only)
e-mail: info@hkcanada.com

Europe: Human Kinetics
107 Bradford Road
Stanningley
Leeds LS28 6AT, United Kingdom
+44 (0) 113 255 5665
e-mail: hk@hkeurope.com

Australia: Human Kinetics
57A Price Avenue
Lower Mitcham, South Australia 5062
08 8372 0999
e-mail: info@hkaustralia.com

New Zealand: Human Kinetics
P.O. Box 80
Mitcham Shopping Centre, South Australia 5062
0800 222 062
e-mail: info@hknewzealand.com

                                                                                          E6307

To my loving and supportive family. Together, we have shared more than a decade of medical coverage with the Chicago Bulls organization and attended hundreds of games with my wife, Emily, and our children, Ethan, Adam, and Ava. I am grateful to have the privilege to always be a student and to add balance to our fulfilling lives.

Brian Cole

To my wife, Dora, and my daughters, Lauren and Sara. Thank you for your love and support throughout the years. You are the roses in my life's bouquet.

Rob Panariello

CONTENTS

FOREWORD

by Derrick Rose

I want to first say that it's an honor to be approached about providing the foreword for Dr. Cole and Rob Panariello's landmark book *Basketball Anatomy.* I truly believe that the content of this resource has had a significant impact on where I am today in my career. I'm also certain that it will have a similar impact on the game's future players, coaches, and trainers.

Basketball has always been an important part of my life. Growing up in Chicago, the game was my way of avoiding the streets and the negative influences that such a lifestyle can have on a young man or woman. I owe a lot of credit to my brothers for teaching me the game at an early age and seeing that I was in position to succeed at the high school level. While I was at Simeon Academy, I was fortunate enough to experience even greater success. The hard work and dedication that I put in every day helped me attract the attention of some of the nation's top college basketball programs and eventually led me to the University of Memphis, where I had the opportunity to play for an NCAA National Championship. Good fortune continued to shine down on me, as after declaring for the 2008 NBA draft, I was the overall first selection by my hometown Chicago Bulls and experienced immediate success in my first few years.

So why do I tell you all of this? Trust me, I am not using this as a way to boast my personal accolades. Things were going great until my first major setback—a serious knee injury. In 2012, while playing in the first game of the NBA Playoffs, I suffered a torn ACL. The timing couldn't have been worse as I didn't have enough time to recover before the following season, which meant that I had to endure not only the pain of the injury, but also having to watch my teammates battle without me. Upon my return at the beginning of the 2013-14 season, I was finally starting to get back into game shape and feeling comfortable again. Then, on November 22nd, the unthinkable happened and again I suffered a season-ending injury. This time a torn meniscus on my other knee. An entire career with no major injury and now I suffer two within a three-year span.

But while I suffered these injuries and it did cost me time out of my career, I was lucky enough to be under the care of Dr. Brian Cole and his team. He knows the game and its demands on the body. That expertise helped me recover from both devastating injuries, and I am now ready to return to the game stronger than ever. The exercises that he and Rob Panariello have included in this book are essential to preparing your body for basketball-specific actions. They even include much of the same injury recovery that I had to endure while recovering from my ACL surgery. You'll learn how to be a better, stronger, healthier player and avoid common injuries in the game. The bottom line is this: When it comes to training basketball players, keeping us healthy, or helping us return from injury, there are no two guys better than Dr. Cole and Rob Panariello. By picking up this resource, you'll learn the same exercises that NBA players use on a daily basis to keep us on the court and not the bench and how each of them directly relates to basketball movements. I've never seen a book that takes you inside the game and shows you why you train—the value, the benefit, and the results. It's my go-to resource and a must for every player coach, trainer, and fan!

PREFACE

D r. Naismith, the creator of the game of shooting balls into peach baskets, could not have dreamed that his game would evolve so dramatically. Though basketball has changed over the past 100-plus years, the spirit and principles of the game remain the same.

From the playground to professional levels, the sport is more popular now than ever before. Every March, fans in the United States watch as a new national collegiate champion is crowned. Later that spring, all eyes are on the best basketball athletes in the world as a new NBA champion is named.

The game of basketball requires various physical qualities for consistent success. Strength, power, and elasticity provide you with the ability to demonstrate your best game. As you commit more time and effort to the sport, your performance will improve as will your ability to prevent and manage injury, and, if necessary, rehabilitate from injury.

Chapter 1 introduces the physical qualities necessary for playing basketball and the correlation of those physical qualities to optimal performance. Chapters 2 through 7 contain detailed exercises with full-color anatomical illustrations aiding in establishing skills such as gaining a strong position, improving jumping skills, getting a quicker first step, and increasing acceleration. Chapter 8 covers the rehabilitation of ankle sprains, knee tendinitis, and shoulder pathology. Chapter 9 describes methods of preventing ACL and shoulder injuries, and chapter 10 describes optimal design of training programs. This systematic method of training will help you prevent overtraining and avoid overuse injuries that often occur as the result of excessive fatigue during weight room training (the key below shows you how to distinguish between primary and secondary muscles in the diagrams).

Motivation for participation in basketball may include seeking simple recreational enjoyment, satisfying the thirst of competition, achieving a college scholarship, and even making it the professional ranks. *Basketball Anatomy* contains the keys that have led to the success of many basketball athletes over the years, all based on authoritative literature and empirical experience. By sharing this information with you, we hope to enhance your physical abilities and help you achieve consistent play and a healthy career.

ACKNOWLEDGMENTS

We would like to thank the following individuals for their hard work and dedication in helping with *Basketball Anatomy:*

Timothy J. Stump MS, PT, CSCS is a licensed physical therapist and NSCA certified strength and conditioning specialist. He received his masters of science degree in exercise physiology and is certified by USA Weightlifting as a club coach and sports performance coach. Tim began his physical therapy career working at the Hospital for Special Surgery in 1992 and then in 2000 he joined Rob Panariello as a partner with Professional Orthopedic and Sports Physical Therapy private practice.

Dean Maddalone PTA, CSCS is an NSCA certified strength & conditioning specialist, USAW weightlifting coach as well as a New York State licensed physical therapist assistant. He is currently the director of athletic performance at the Professional Athletic Performance Center in Garden City, New York. Dean has worked in outpatient sports medicine for more than 20 years and has performance trained and rehabilitated many high school, college, and professional basketball and baseball athletes.

Jessica Paparella DPT, PT is a physical therapist and clinical director with Professional Orthopedic and Sports Physical Therapy in Garden City, New York. Jessica graduated from Stony Brook University's physical therapy program in 2009. She is a former collegiate softball player and has a special interest in the area of sports physical therapy and concussion management, and she is also involved in the care of athletes at all levels of competition including the NHL and MLB.

chapter 1

THE BASKETBALL PLAYER IN MOTION

Participation in basketball, as in any other athletic endeavor, requires athletes to optimize all of the contributing physical qualities to ensure their best athletic efforts will occur repeatedly over time. Basketball players must be able to run, jump, accelerate, decelerate, and change direction. A common thread to the success of these physical tasks is to be efficient from the ground up; in other words, you must apply optimal levels of force into the floor in the shortest time. Sir Isaac Newton's third law of motion states that for every action there is an equal and opposite reaction. Therefore, the more force you can apply to the ground, the greater the reaction force that will be applied back from the ground to propel you. Elite athletes are those who place the greatest amount of force into the floor in the least time. To improve your ability to rapidly apply high levels of force into the floor, you must enhance specific physical qualities in a specific sequence.

SKILL VERSUS ATHLETICISM

In discussing athletic performance enhancement, there is often confusion in differentiating level of athleticism from level of skill. When discussing the physical training process, both coaches and athletes need to be familiar with these distinctions.

A skill specific to basketball is the jump shot, a key offensive weapon and a critical aspect in scoring points during a game. An example of basketball athleticism is the ability to jump high. Although the skill of jump shooting and the athleticism of jumping high are related, they also are different. You might train to increase your vertical jump, but this does not ensure that you will improve accuracy in jump shots. To become a better jump shooter, you must practice the skill of jump shooting. The ability to jump high (athleticism) may help you avoid a defender's outstretched hand, but your proficiency in making the jump shot will improve only by practicing the jump shot.

When training to enhance the physical qualities necessary for basketball, you work to improve athleticism. Actually practicing and playing basketball enhances basketball skills. The repetitive practice of basketball skills performed over time will bring about physical improvement.

PHYSICAL QUALITIES OF BASKETBALL ATHLETES

The physical qualities necessary for high levels of athletic performance, regardless of the sport, are strength, power (explosive strength), elastic (reactive) strength, and speed. The optimal development of each physical quality depends on the most favorable development of the preceding physical quality. The hierarchy of athletic development (figure 1.1) was established by former San Francisco 49ers and Chicago Bulls Hall of Fame strength and conditioning coach Al Vermeil.

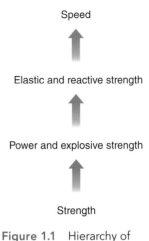

Speed

↑

Elastic and reactive strength

↑

Power and explosive strength

↑

Strength

Figure 1.1   Hierarchy of athletic development.

Modified from an illustration created by Al Vermeil. Used with permission.

PHYSICAL ADAPTATION AND TRAINING

One component of the athletic training program is the application of appropriate levels of stress which are crucial for adaptation (improvement). This adaptation by the body is vital for developing various physical qualities in preparation for competition.

The fundamental model of training, as well as the ensuing adaptation process, is derived from the general adaptation syndrome (GAS) initially outlined by Hans Selye in 1936 and later refined by Selye in 1956. The fundamental model concept is also known in the literature as the supercompensation cycle. This stress response model (figure 1.2) is initiated by an alarm phase as a training stimulus (application of stress), which results in disruption of homeostasis of the body.

The body responds to the stimulus in the resistance phase by recovering and repairing itself while prompting a return toward the baseline of homeostasis. The resistance phase is followed by a period of supercompensation, during which the body adapts to the initially applied stimulus by rebounding above the previous homeostasis baseline in order to better manage the initially applied disruptive stress should it present itself once again.

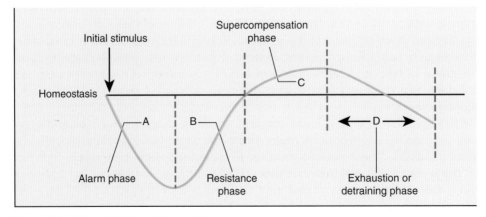

Figure 1.2   General adaptation syndrome.

The exhaustion (detraining) phase ensues with a reduction of the body's initial level, below the level of homeostasis, as a result of an improper application of a stressful stimulus such as too much too soon or an inadequate level of applied stress. It's beneficial to familiarize yourself with Selye's general adaptation syndrome. See his work, *The Stress of Life* (1956).

Based on this GAS model, it's easy to see the necessity for unaccustomed stress—weight intensities, jump heights, running speeds—so that you can adapt and improve the physical qualities. According to these principles, assume that you require a certain level of stress in order to disrupt your homeostasis for an adaptation (training effect) to occur. If the stress applied during training is too low, little, if any, physical adaptation will take place, resulting in a loss of valuable training time. For this reason, you should be assessed for physical deficits, physical needs, and goals so that you can design and implement an appropriate physical training program.

STRENGTH

In Al Vermeil's hierarchy of athletic development (figure 1.1), strength is the quality from which all others are derived. When the athleticism and skill levels of two opposing athletes are the same, the stronger athlete usually will prevail.

Strength is the ability of a muscle to produce maximal force, which is developed when you progressively incorporate higher levels of exercise intensity (weight to be lifted). Since higher levels of exercise intensity are more demanding on the body, one unique component to strength training is that there is no time requirement to complete the exercise. Heavier weights are lifted at a slower velocity; a faster exercise performance is used when incorporating lighter weights. Exercises commonly used to enhance the physical quality of strength are discussed in chapters 2 through 5.

With regard to basketball performance, the quality of strength is important for the development of both the soft tissues of the body (muscle, ligament, and tendon), as stated in Davis' law, as well as the osseous structures of the body (bone), as stated in Wolff's law. The improved qualities of these anatomical structures is important for basketball performance because enhanced force output by a muscle or muscle group will result in a higher application of force to the floor. This will improve your ability to accelerate, run fast, and jump high. Stronger soft tissues and stronger bone also assist in your ability to decelerate and change direction as well as prevent injury during practice and competition.

Enhanced levels of strength also result in improved levels of muscle and joint stiffness. This improvement is not to be confused with the loss of motion at the anatomical joints of the body or loss of flexibility. Certain amounts of muscle and joint stiffness are necessary for maintaining optimal posture during running, jumping, and other basketball activities. For example, when landing from an offensive rebound and immediately jumping to reshoot the ball, you would not want your body to collapse, so to speak. The more the ankles, knees, hips, and torso flex on landing, the more time you spend on the floor, making more time available for the defense to recover before another shot. Higher levels of muscle and joint stiffness reduce the amount of anatomical joint flexing and bending on landing, resulting in less time spent on the floor, more force applied to the floor, and a higher jump when you reshoot the ball.

POWER AND EXPLOSIVE STRENGTH

Basketball is a game of jumping, acceleration, deceleration, and quickness. All these movements require rapid velocities. If you move slowly, you will not be very successful during competition.

While the physical quality of strength is the foundation for athletic performance, the higher exercise intensities that occur with strength training encompass slower movements during training. Although strength development has no time limit during exercise performance, power and explosive strength do encompass a factor of time for the conclusion of the exercise performance. Power and explosive strength involve the ability to turn on the strength (muscular force) available very quickly as these types of exercises are performed at higher velocities. These exercises depend more on the muscles' rate of force development (RFD).

The RFD determines the amount of force a muscle can generate in a very brief time. During athletic competition, the time available for this generated force to occur is very short, usually 200 to 300 milliseconds. Think of a basketball player who beats his opponent on the first step with a drive to the basket or a player who demonstrates a high vertical jump. Do these athletes' muscles fire at slow or high velocities? Figure 1.3 compares two athletes when considering time as a factor in ability to produce muscular force. Athlete A (red line) is stronger than the more explosive one, athlete B (yellow line). Although the stronger athlete (red line) produces a greater muscular force over time (500 ms), this stronger athlete also produces less force at the shorter period (the dotted line at 200 ms).

Strength training sets the stage and contributes to the initial enhancement of RFD, but other proven methods enhance power. These training methods are discussed in chapters 6 and 7.

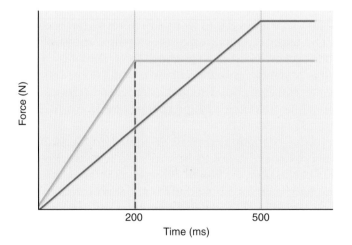

Figure 1.3 Comparison of rate of force development in two athletes.

ELASTIC AND REACTIVE STRENGTH

Prestretching a tendon before performing an athletic task results in a more forceful and explosive concentric (shortening) muscle contraction. For example, lay your right hand flat on a table. Actively raise your index finger as high as possible and then hit the table surface as hard as you can. Repeat the task by using your left index finger to pull the right index finger back as far as safely possible without injuring yourself. Release your right index finger and hit the table surface as hard as possible. Do you hear a difference in the sound of the force of impact? The difference between these two active attempts is that, in the second attempt, the tendons and muscles of the right index finger were prestretched before the finger hit the table surface, resulting in a more forceful impact. Placing the muscles and tendons in a prestretched position before performing a concentric muscle contraction results in a more forceful concentric muscle contraction. This is the reason athletes place their bodies in a prestretch position before performing an athletic skill. They quickly and slightly squat before jumping, wind up before throwing, and cock the leg back before kicking an object.

This prestretch phenomenon is due to the stretch–shortening cycle (SSC) of muscles and tendons. The SSC describes an eccentric (lengthening) muscle contraction (stretch) before the initiation of the explosive concentric (shortening) muscle contraction. The SSC is synonymous with the term *plyometrics* and is discussed in detail in chapter 7.

SPEED

When speed is discussed with regard to athletes, usually it is in terms of the top speed demonstrated by an Olympic 100-meter sprinter or a football player running down the field. These athletes perform on larger fields of play (as opposed to a basketball court, which is 94 feet by 50 feet) so they are able to reach their maximum velocity. Because of the limited playing area of a basketball court, in addition to the confrontation of a defensive opponent, speed is a physical quality not often demonstrated in a basketball game and thus not emphasized in this book.

CONCLUSION

Not only are the physical qualities described in this chapter important for optimal basketball play, but the sequence of the development of each of these physical qualities is important as well. The guidelines for basketball training are discussed in chapter 10. Proper training will help prevent injuries, but sometimes injuries do occur. Chapter 8 covers injury rehabilitation and return to play; chapter 9 covers injury prevention.

chapter 2

LEGS: WHERE THE GAME STARTS

The majority of, if not all, athletic endeavors are initiated by the application of forces from the ground up, and the game of basketball is no different. The elite athletes of the world are those who apply the greatest amount of force into the ground surface area in the shortest period of time. Lower-extremity strength is a vital physical component to the application of force for optimal performance (see figure 2.1). Strength is also important for recovery from the initial force output in situations such as landing from a high vertical jump or decelerating before cutting. You must run, jump, accelerate, decelerate, and cut at high velocities because these tasks are both initiated by and dependent on the strength in the lower extremities. The legs are considered the foundation from which all basketball skills evolve, so you know how important lower-extremity strength is to the sport.

In review of Al Vermeil's hierarchy of athletic development, strength is the foundation from which all other physical qualities develop. When referring to strength development in basketball players, remember that we are not speaking of the strength levels of weightlifters, powerlifters, or bodybuilders, because those athletes develop strength for their specific competitive goals. In training for basketball, your goal is not to become a weightlifter; rather, it is to use strength training exercises to enhance the physical qualities with the goal of improving athleticism and performance.

Strength is the groundwork for muscle function, hypertrophy, and force output as well as the enhancement of bone density and tendon and ligament stability. These anatomical structures must resist the physical stresses that occur during the game of basketball. Enhancing the strength of the soft tissues and bony structures of the legs will support your armor coat, so to speak, and help prevent injuries. In basketball, the most common injuries of the lower extremities are to the soft tissues (muscles, tendons, and ligaments) and joints. You must produce high forces to run, jump, and cut as well as to recover. In other words, you must generate forces opposing the forces produced for body propulsion in order to decelerate before a change of direction and land safely from a high vertical jump. If you are not able to slow down from these high forces, injury is likely to occur. During the game these output and braking forces are repeated over prolonged periods.

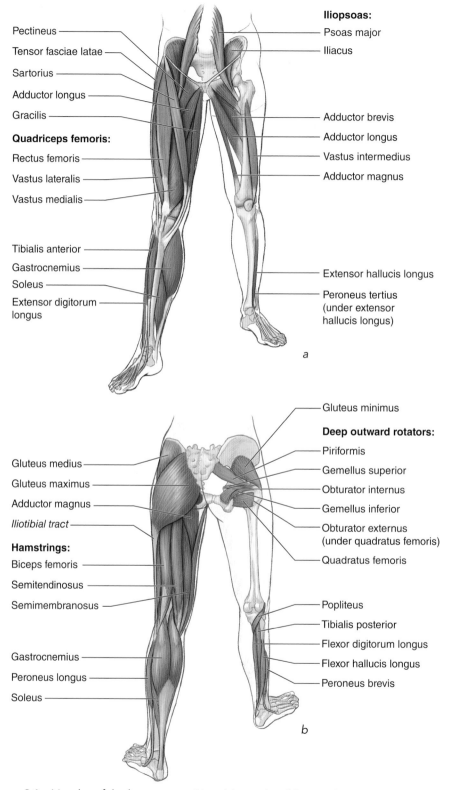

Pectineus

Tensor fasciae latae

Sartorius

Adductor longus

Gracilis

Quadriceps femoris:

Rectus femoris

Vastus lateralis

Vastus medialis

Tibialis anterior

Gastrocnemius

Soleus

Extensor digitorum
longus

Iliopsoas:

Psoas major

Iliacus

Adductor brevis

Adductor longus

Vastus intermedius

Adductor magnus

Extensor hallucis longus

Peroneus tertius
(under extensor
hallucis longus)

a

Gluteus minimus

Deep outward rotators:

Piriformis

Gemellus superior

Obturator internus

Gemellus inferior

Obturator externus
(under quadratus femoris)

Quadratus femoris

Gluteus medius

Gluteus maximus

Adductor magnus

Iliotibial tract

Hamstrings:

Biceps femoris

Semitendinosus

Semimembranosus

Gastrocnemius

Peroneus longus

Soleus

Popliteus

Tibialis posterior

Flexor digitorum longus

Flexor hallucis longus

Peroneus brevis

b

Figure 2.1   Muscles of the lower extremities: *(a)* anterior; *(b)* posterior.

Weak muscles and soft tissue structures fatigue easily and therefore eventually become more dependent on joint structures to assist in the absorption of high-energy forces. Although the joints are able to absorb some of the forces produced in basketball, they are not equipped to absorb the majority of these high forces repeatedly over time. As a result, injuries occur. Players who are injured require recovery, during which they should not participate in games. Strengthening the muscles of the lower extremities not only will assist in enhancing athletic abilities, but also will enable you to demonstrate those abilities repeatedly over time while resisting injuries. To ensure proper technique, perform the strength exercises described in this chapter with light weights before increasing the weight.

Following are the strength exercises described in this chapter:

Back squat

Front squat

Deadlift

Romanian deadlift (RDL)

Hip thrust

Reverse lunge

Reverse step-down from box

Band backward walk

Band lateral walk

Calf pop-up

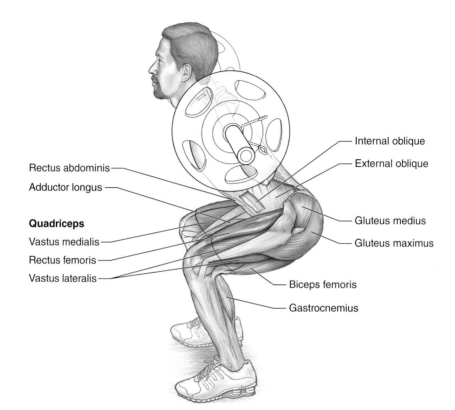

Internal oblique

External oblique

Rectus abdominis

Adductor longus

Quadriceps

Vastus medialis

Rectus femoris

Vastus lateralis

Gluteus medius

Gluteus maximus

Biceps femoris

Gastrocnemius

Execution

1. Stand erect and place a barbell behind your neck on the upper trapezius with the weight evenly distributed across the shoulders. Feet are slightly wider than shoulder width and outwardly rotated approximately 15 degrees.

2. Keeping the back as straight as possible, slowly descend by bending at the hips and knees until the thighs are slightly lower than parallel to the floor. During the descent, keep the elbows down and in line with your trunk. There will be some flexion of the trunk to maintain the barbell over the base of support. The trunk should hinge on the pelvis while the spine maintains a neutral posture.

3. Without bouncing at the bottom position, change direction by extending the hips and knees to ascend to the starting position.

Muscles Involved

Primary: Gluteus maximus, gluteus medius, hamstrings (semitendinosus, semi-membranosus, biceps femoris), quadriceps (rectus femoris, vastus lateralis, vastus medialis, vastus intermedius)

Secondary: Erector spinae (iliocostalis, longissimus, spinalis), rectus abdominis, external oblique, internal oblique, adductor longus, adductor brevis, gastrocnemius

Basketball Focus

The squat has long been noted as the king of exercises among strength and conditioning professionals. This exercise enhances the musculature of the legs, hips, low back, and abdomen. Enhanced strength in these muscle groups will allow you to apply optimal levels of force into the floor, resulting in improved acceleration and jumping ability. Enhancement of strength in the lower extremity will also provide additional stability when positioning either offensively or defensively by boxing out the opponent in preparation for receiving the basketball and rebounding.

FRONT SQUAT

Starting position.

Quadriceps:
Vastus lateralis
Rectus femoris
Vastus medialis
Adductor longus
Hamstrings:
Semimembranosus
Semitendinosus

External oblique
Rectus abdominis
Gluteus medius
Gluteus maximus
Biceps femoris
Gastrocnemius

Execution

1. Stand erect with a barbell in front of the neck across the deltoid muscles with the weight evenly distributed across the shoulders. Two grips are recommended. The first is the Olympic-style grip: Hold the bar in the fingers with the elbows raised parallel to the floor. This grip requires wrist flexibility. This grip is used in catching the bar during Olympic-style power exercises. The second and easier way to hold the barbell is with the cross grip. With the palms down, the right hand holds the barbell at the left deltoid and the left hand holds the barbell at the right deltoid. The elbows remain raised to shoulder level during the exercise.

2. As in the back squat, keep the back as straight as possible while slowly descending by bending at the hips and knees until the thighs are slightly lower than parallel to the floor. During the descent, keep the elbows up and in line with the shoulders.

3. Achieve the bottom position of the exercise without bouncing and change direction by extending the hips and knees to ascend to the starting position.

Muscles Involved

Primary: Gluteus maximus, gluteus medius, hamstrings (semitendinosus, semimembranosus, biceps femoris), quadriceps (rectus femoris, vastus lateralis, vastus medialis, vastus intermedius)

Secondary: Erector spinae (iliocostalis, longissimus, spinalis), rectus abdominis, external oblique, internal oblique, adductor longus, adductor brevis, gastrocnemius

Basketball Focus

Because of the positioning of the barbell in front of the body, the front squat allows for a more erect body position during execution. This erect body position places less stress on the low back muscles and works the quadriceps more than the back squat exercise does. Generally the front squat is performed with approximately 20 percent less weight compared to the back squat.

Like the back squat, the front squat is an important basketball-related exercise. It develops the strength of the low back, hips, and lower extremities for optimal force output and deceleration, which are very important for acceleration and cutting during play. The ability to beat your opponent to the basket will depend on your ability to accelerate, decelerate, and change direction.

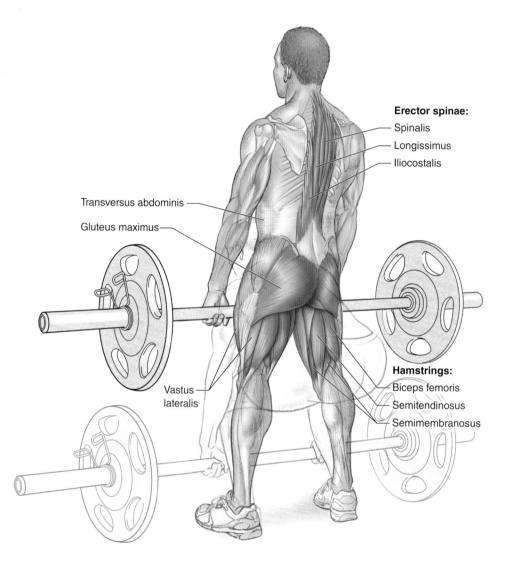

Erector spinae:
Spinalis
Longissimus
Iliocostalis

Transversus abdominis

Gluteus maximus

Hamstrings:
Biceps femoris
Semitendinosus
Semimembranosus

Vastus
lateralis

Execution

1. Stand over a barbell on the floor with the bar positioned above the midfoot. The feet are slightly narrower than shoulder-width to provide room for the arms during execution.

2. Grip the barbell with the arms straight and perpendicular to the floor, shoulders slightly over the bar, and hands positioned outside the legs. Use a reverse grip (grip the bar with one hand palm down and the other hand palm up).

3. Slowly bend the hips and knees while keeping the back straight to lower your body until your shins touch the bar while it remains at the midfoot position. Raise your shoulders to straighten your arms as your head remains in line with your neutrally positioned spine.

4. Pull the bar from the floor by slowly extending the hips and knees as the shoulders simultaneously rise with the hips. Keep the arms and back straight; do not let the back round. Maintain a close position of the barbell to the body until you stand erect.

5. Return the bar to the floor by slowly flexing the hips and then the knees, controlling the bar until it touches the floor.

Muscles Involved

Primary: Gluteus maximus, erector spinae (iliocostalis, longissimus, spinalis), hamstrings (semitendinosus, semimembranosus, biceps femoris)

Secondary: Rectus abdominis, transversus abdominis, quadriceps (rectus femoris, vastus lateralis, vastus medialis, vastus intermedius), iliopsoas

Basketball Focus

As with the back squat and front squat, the deadlift is a multijoint exercise that allows you to exercise with optimal weight. This exercise enhances strength in the low back, hip, and lower extremity. These muscle groups are important for force output, enhancing acceleration, and jumping, which are components of a successful layup. This exercise enhances deceleration and cutting and improves your base of support, which helps you achieve an optimal position of stability for boxing out, receiving the basketball, rebounding, and playing under the basket.

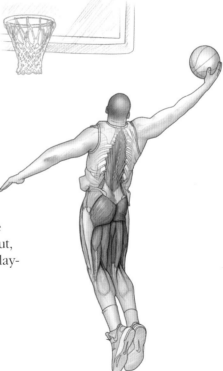

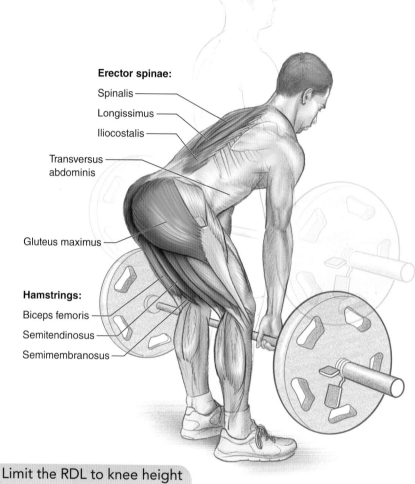

Erector spinae:
Spinalis
Longissimus
Iliocostalis

Transversus
abdominis

Gluteus maximus

Hamstrings:
Biceps femoris
Semitendinosus
Semimembranosus

SAFETY TIP ▷ Limit the RDL to knee height until you achieve proper technique and enhanced hamstring flexibility.

Execution

1. Unlike the deadlift, the RDL does not start from the floor but is performed from the top down, so to speak. Stand erect with the arms straight, holding a barbell with an overhand (palms down) grip. Stand with feet approximately hip-width apart with the toes pointing straight ahead or slightly turned out (up to 15 degrees). The barbell should touch the thighs. Slightly flex the knees to 20 or 30 degrees.

2. Keeping the low back (spine) and knees locked at this slightly flexed position, lower the bar slowly against the thighs by extending the hips back as if on a hinge while allowing the torso to drop. Do not round the back or shoulders as the bar lowers via the movement of the hips extending back, not via the movement of the waist flexing forward.

3. Return the bar to the starting position by keeping the shoulders, knees, and low back locked as the hips extend forward until you are standing upright.

Muscles Involved

Primary: Gluteus maximus, hamstrings (semitendinosus, semimembranosus, biceps femoris), erector spinae (iliocostalis, longissimus, spinalis)

Secondary: Rectus abdominis, transversus abdominis, iliopsoas

Basketball Focus

Like the other lower-extremity strength exercises, the RDL enhances the force output for running, jumping, decelerating, cutting, and maintaining proper ratios of posterior and anterior thigh strength to assist in preventing muscle strains and ligament injuries. By increasing the strength of the lower back and hips, you are better prepared to establish a defensive position and reactive movement as you guard an opponent while traveling up the basketball court.

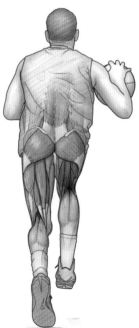

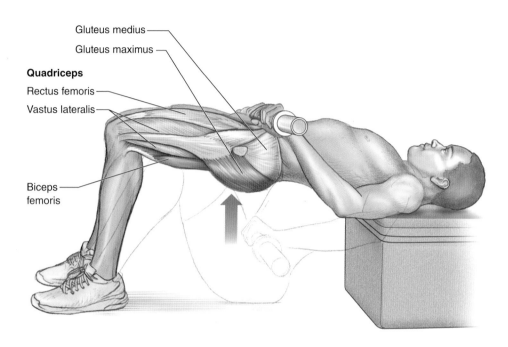

LEG STRENGTH

Gluteus medius

Gluteus maximus

Quadriceps

Rectus femoris

Vastus lateralis

Biceps femoris

Execution

1. Sit with the hips on the floor and both legs extended. Align the upper back across a secure padded bench or box. Position a well-padded barbell over the lower legs.

2. Lean forward to grab the barbell and, if the size of the weight plates allow, roll the barbell over the thighs toward the hips. The barbell is positioned symmetrically at the crease of the hips slightly above the pelvis.

3. Lean back to assume proper placement of the upper back and shoulders on the padded bench. Slide your feet toward buttocks, keeping them at shoulder width and keeping the knees flexed to 90 degrees, assuming a vertically positioned tibia.

4. Lift the barbell off the floor by extending the hips using the gluteal muscles while simultaneously keeping the spine and hips in a neutral position (no excessive arching of the back). The extension movement that lifts the bar must come from the hips and not from the low back.

> **SAFETY TIP** The back of the shoulder should have firm support on the padded bench. The cervical spine (neck) should not be the main support during the exercise.

Muscles Involved

Primary: Gluteus maximus, hamstrings (semitendinosus, semimembranosus, biceps femoris), adductor magnus

Secondary: Gluteus medius, gluteus minimus, erector spinae (iliocostalis, longissimus, spinalis), quadriceps (rectus femoris, vastus lateralis, vastus medialis, vastus intermedius)

Basketball Focus

The gluteal muscles significantly contribute to improving horizontal and vertical body propulsion, which is necessary for accelerating past an opponent as well as outjumping an opponent. These muscles are also crucial for safe and efficient landings and contribute to your ability to break away from an opponent via enhanced deceleration and cutting.

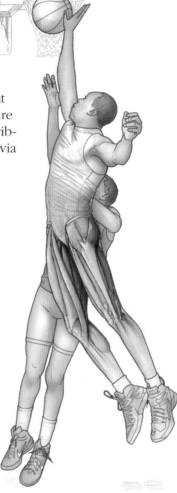

REVERSE LUNGE

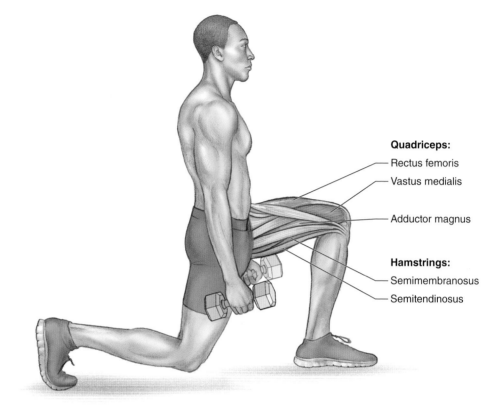

Quadriceps:
Rectus femoris
Vastus medialis

Adductor magnus

Hamstrings:
Semimembranosus
Semitendinosus

Execution

1. You can use the reverse lunge independently or as a lead-up exercise to the reverse step-down from box. Stand erect with your feet shoulder-width apart. You may place your hands on your hips or hold a dumbbell in each hand if you want additional resistance.

2. Step directly back with the right leg and lower the body toward the floor by bending both hips and knees while maintaining an erect posture and vertical tibia on the left (forward) leg. Descend until the left leg is bent 90 degrees at the hip and knee.

3. Return to the starting position. After you complete all repetitions with the right leg back, do the exercise with the left leg back.

Muscles Involved

Primary: Quadriceps (rectus femoris, vastus lateralis, vastus medialis, vastus intermedius), gluteus maximus, gluteus medius

Secondary: Hamstrings (semitendinosus, semimembranosus, biceps femoris), gluteus minimus, adductor magnus

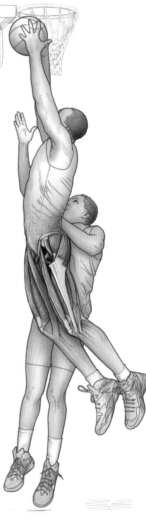

Basketball Focus

This exercise strengthens the muscles of the thighs and hips, which assist with both horizontal and vertical body propulsion as well as enhance your ability to decelerate and change direction to avoid an opponent. Horizontal and vertical propulsion also are necessary for acceleration and jumping. Enhanced deceleration will help you cut and change direction to avoid an opponent. Balance and proprioception are also improved with this exercise. These qualities assist in not only the positioning of the lower extremities in running, cutting, and jumping, but injury prevention as well.

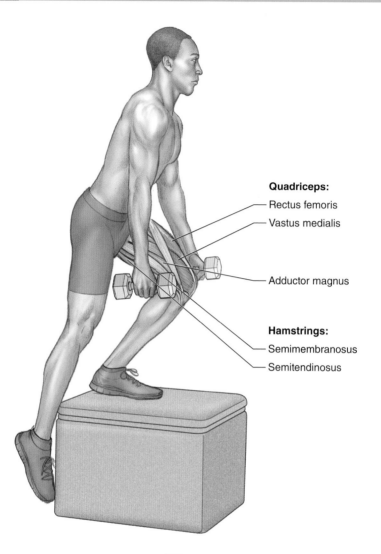

Quadriceps:
Rectus femoris
Vastus medialis

Adductor magnus

Hamstrings:
Semimembranosus
Semitendinosus

SAFETY TIP

During the exercise, be sure to maintain neuromuscular control of the knees; do not let the knees buckle in or out.

Execution

1. Stand with both feet firmly on top of a secure 12- to 24-inch (30-60 cm) box. The height of the box depends on your strength.

2. Keeping the left leg on the box, slowly step back off the box with the right leg with the foot plantar flexed (pointed) toward the floor. Slowly descend toward the floor by bending at the left hip and knee, keeping the trunk as erect as possible while maintaining the pointed foot toward the floor.

3. Touch, don't bounce, off the floor with the toes of the right foot before changing direction. The instant the toes of the right foot touch the floor, extend both hip and knee to return to the straight-leg starting position.

4. Without resting, continue the exercise for the prescribed number of repetitions on the same leg. After completing the repetitions, repeat with the right leg remaining on the box as the left leg steps back off the box.

Muscles Involved

Primary: Quadriceps (rectus femoris, vastus lateralis, vastus medialis, vastus intermedius), gluteus maximus, gluteus medius

Secondary: Hamstrings (semitendinosus, semimembranosus, biceps femoris), gluteus minimus, adductor magnus

Basketball Focus

This single-leg strength exercise assists in both horizontal and vertical body propulsion, which is essential for running past and outjumping an opponent as in taking a layup. This exercise also assists with deceleration from a single-leg position during cutting activities, proprioception, and overall body control, which are important during any violent contact that might occur during play.

BAND BACKWARD WALK

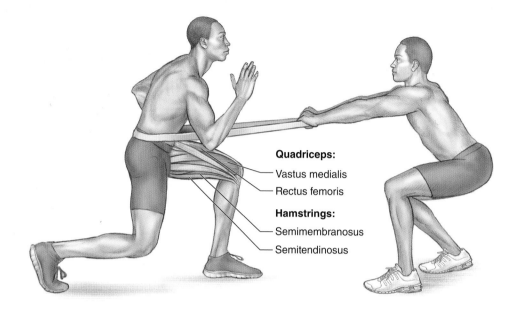

Quadriceps:

Vastus medialis

Rectus femoris

Hamstrings:

Semimembranosus

Semitendinosus

Execution

1. Facing a partner, stand and assume a quarter-squat position with both feet shoulder-width apart. Secure a long, heavy-resistance (rubber) band around your waist. Your partner holds the opposite end of the band.

2. Maintaining proper posture, walk backward against the manual resistance of the band, determined by the partner holding the band, for a prescribed distance. Your partner walks with you while applying the resistance.

3. The exercise is initiated with 25-yard backward walks and progresses to 50-yard backward walks for up to five sets.

Muscles Involved

Primary: Quadriceps (rectus femoris, vastus lateralis, vastus medialis, vastus intermedius), gluteus maximus

Secondary: Hamstrings (semitendinosus, semimembranosus, biceps femoris), gluteus medius

Basketball Focus

This exercise develops strength and endurance of the lower extremities and hips for optimal force output performed repetitively over time. Strength in the quadriceps and hips is important for applying force into the floor, resulting in acceleration and jumping abilities. These muscle groups also play an active role in deceleration, which is important for changing direction when attempting to beat an opponent and landing from a jump. Strength endurance is important as you must demonstrate the ability to perform these athletic endeavors often throughout practice and game performance.

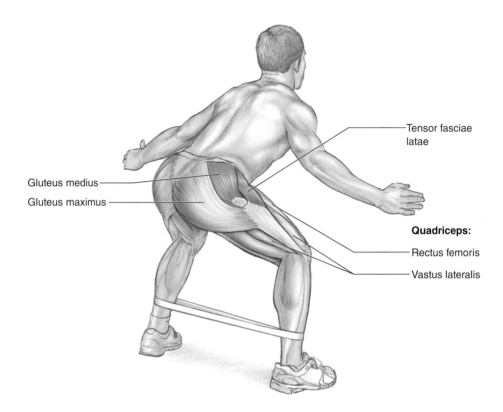

Tensor fasciae latae

Gluteus medius

Gluteus maximus

Quadriceps:

Rectus femoris

Vastus lateralis

Execution

1. Stand and assume a quarter-squat position with feet shoulder-width apart. Loop a miniband of appropriate resistance around each ankle. You may start with the lightest band resistance and increase to the next level of resistance once you're able to complete the required distance or number of repetitions.

2. Step to the left by pushing off the right foot. Do not step to the left by initiating the movement with the left leg moving laterally.

3. On completion of the step to the left, step to the left again, initiating the movement by pushing from the right foot. Repeat the exercise for the prescribed distance.

4. Return to the starting position by performing the exercise to the right, initiating each step by pushing the left foot. Begin the exercise with 25-yard lateral walks and progress to 50-yard lateral walks for up to five sets.

Muscles Involved

Primary: Gluteus medius, gluteus minimus, tensor fasciae latae

Secondary: Gluteus maximus, quadriceps (rectus femoris, vastus lateralis, vastus medialis, vastus intermedius)

Basketball Focus

This exercise increases lateral hip and thigh strength to assist in rapidly changing direction when dribbling. This ability will help you beat the defender whether you are establishing a position on the court or driving to the basket for a layup.

CALF POP-UP

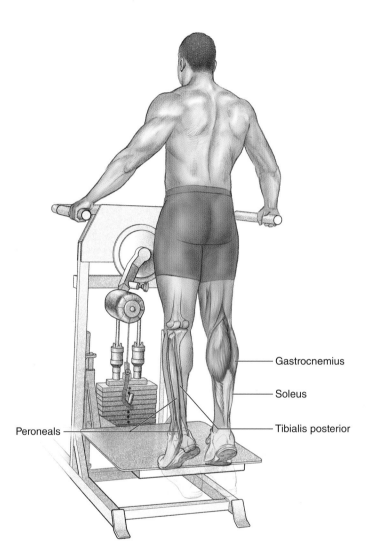

Gastrocnemius

Soleus

Peroneals

Tibialis posterior

Execution

1. Stand erect with the balls of both feet on the edge of a secure flat surface. Hold on to a fixed structure with both hands to maintain balance.

2. Slowly lower both heels toward the floor as you stretch your Achilles tendons.

3. Reverse direction to quickly pop up onto your toes.

4. Perform the prescribed number of repetitions.

Muscles Involved

Primary: Gastrocnemius, soleus

Secondary: Tibialis posterior, peroneals

Basketball Focus

Enhancing the strength of the gastrocnemius, soleus, and Achilles tendon complex will help you jump higher during shooting and rebounding skills. Strengthening this muscle-tendon complex will also enhance the elasticity of the Achilles tendon, which will give you a distinct advantage over an opponent. You may take a jump shot, miss the shot, and jump again for a rebound immediately after landing. As a defender, you will jump to block the jump shot and jump for the rebound immediately after landing. Enhancing the strength of this muscle tendon complex correlates to an increase in elasticity so you can jump higher than your opponent on the subsequent second jump.

chapter 3

LOWER BACK AND CORE: THE CENTER OF STABILITY

Over the past several years, *core* has become a buzzword describing the trunk and associated muscles of the midsection. The truth is a little more complicated, but when focusing on increasing strength on the basketball court, it is best to consider the core the part of the body that connects to the force generated by the lower body and transfers that force to the upper body. Without a strong core, you will lack much in terms of sport performance.

The core can be broken down into two basic categories: the inner core and the outer core. The inner core's purpose is stability. It stabilizes the midsection to ensure proper posture and provide a stable platform. This affords you the stability to support the torso during running, jumping, and landing. The outer core produces spinal movement in a variety of planes. This gives you the strength to extend the spine and hips while jumping and produces torque when twisting to strip a ball or pivoting while dribbling.

The inner core is composed of the transversus abdominis, transversospinalis group, pelvic floor muscles, and diaphragm (figure 3.1). These muscles are difficult to conceptualize because they are not always visible on the surface anatomy. The transversus abdominis and muscles of the transversospinalis group function synergistically. The transversus abdominis produces a corsetlike effect for the abdominal cavity. The transversospinalis group includes the multifidus and rotators. These smaller muscles span only a few vertebral segments and add to the stability of the spine by resisting torque and enhancing your postural awareness.

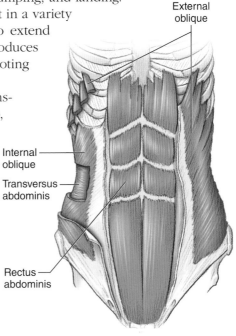

Figure 3.1 Abdominal muscles.

External oblique

Internal oblique

Transversus abdominis

Rectus abdominis

These two muscle groups of the inner core work together to stabilize the entire spinal column and reduce the risk of injury.

The outer core is composed of the rectus abdominis, erector spinae group (iliocostalis, longissimus, and spinalis), and internal and external obliques (figure 3.2). This group of muscles is responsible for producing and resisting movement on the court, as in a low post position under the basket. One way to think of these muscle groups is a part of a kinetic chain. The links in this human chain are responsible for producing movement in various planes. For example, the rectus abdominis coupled with the hip flexors make up the anterior chain, while the erector spinae coupled with the hamstrings and glutes make up the powerful posterior chain. The obliques are responsible for trunk rotation and lateral flexion.

To fully develop the strong and stable core necessary for playing basketball, you need to strengthen all the muscles responsible for producing or resisting movement in various planes. You need to choose an exercise from each movement category for optimal muscle balance and sport performance. We chose four of the most basketball-specific core exercises for training our athletes.

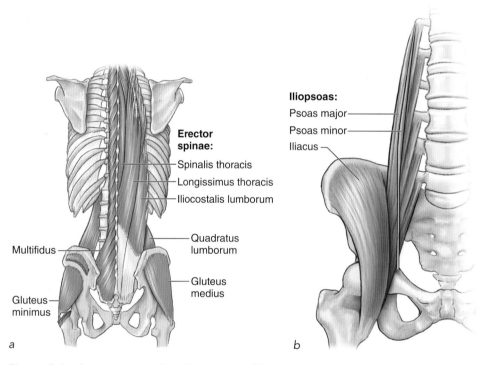

Figure 3.2 Outer core muscles: *(a)* posterior; *(b)* anterior.

Following are the exercises in this chapter:

Core Flexion

Banana
Supine basketball core pass

Core Extension

Back extension
Quadruped arm and leg lift (bird dog)

Core Rotation

Horizontal cable core (Pallof) press
Landmine trunk rotation

Core Lateral Flexion

Lateral plank
Overhead cable core press

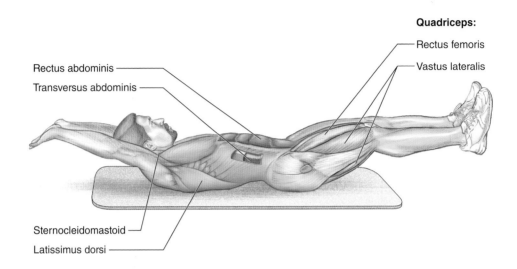

Quadriceps:

Rectus femoris

Vastus lateralis

Rectus abdominis

Transversus abdominis

Sternocleidomastoid

Latissimus dorsi

Execution

1. Lie supine on the floor with legs together, arms extended overhead, and navel pulled in toward spine. This process is referred to as drawing in the abdominals and activates the transversus abdominis.

2. Keeping the head between the arms, slowly raise the upper body and legs off the floor to form a gentle bananalike curve. Hold for a slow 30 counts. Don't hold your breath! Try to keep breathing steady and even. The important part of this drill is to concentrate on holding in the abs, thus not letting your back arch away from the floor.

3. Slowly return to a flat supine position with the arms, head, and legs resting comfortably on the floor.

4. Perform the prescribed number of repetitions.

Muscles Involved

Primary: Rectus abdominis, transversus abdominis

Secondary: Iliopsoas, sartorius, quadriceps (rectus femoris, vastus lateralis, vastus medialis, vastus intermedius), latissimus dorsi, sternocleidomastoid

Basketball Focus

The banana is probably the most underestimated of the core exercises. It seems easy but it is extremely difficult to perform correctly. This exercise adds to the stability of the trunk musculature when you are in a fully extended position. Think of how beneficial it would be to have a stable trunk and core when jumping up for a rebound or jump ball. A strong and stable trunk allows you to sustain the rigors of contact under the boards and when jumping for a rebound.

⟨ VARIATION ⟩

Rock and Roll

One way to make this exercise more challenging is by adding some mild motion. Gently rocking back and forth from head to toe will increase the demands on the anterior chain muscles, the rectus abdominis, and transversus abdominis. Or roll a quarter turn on your side and hold. This will add a bit of complexity because it engages the internal and external obliques as well.

SUPINE BASKETBALL CORE PASS

Extend.

Triceps brachii

Rectus abdominis

Latissimus dorsi

Transversus abdominis

Quadriceps:

Rectus femoris

Vastus lateralis

Sartorius

Pass.

Execution

1. Lie supine on the floor with the legs straight out and together, arms extended overhead, and navel pulled in toward the spine. Hold a basketball in both hands.

2. Sit up with arms straight overhead and pass the basketball from your hands to between your feet.

3. Return to lying flat on your back while maintaining your abdominal draw-in. Squeeze the ball between your feet and lift your legs and pelvis up to pass the ball back to your hands.

4. Slowly return to a flat supine position with the arms, head, and legs resting comfortably on the floor.

5. Perform the prescribed number of repetitions.

Muscles Involved

Primary: Rectus abdominis, transversus abdominis, iliopsoas, latissimus dorsi

Secondary: Sartorius, quadriceps (rectus femoris, vastus lateralis, vastus medialis, vastus intermedius), triceps brachii

Basketball Focus

Not only is this an excellent core exercise, but it also keeps you engaged because you use a basketball during the exercise. This may be mentally stimulating for you and keep you motivated while performing a productive exercise, ultimately improving compliance with the program. Using a basketball as part of the exercise can stimulate the muscles required for passing during a game. As the motion of the ball begins, you must engage the trunk muscles to stabilize the upper body and generate enough force to throw the ball.

⟨ VARIATION ⟩

Weighted-Ball Pass

Increase the demand of the exercise by using a weighted medicine ball instead of a basketball.

BACK EXTENSION

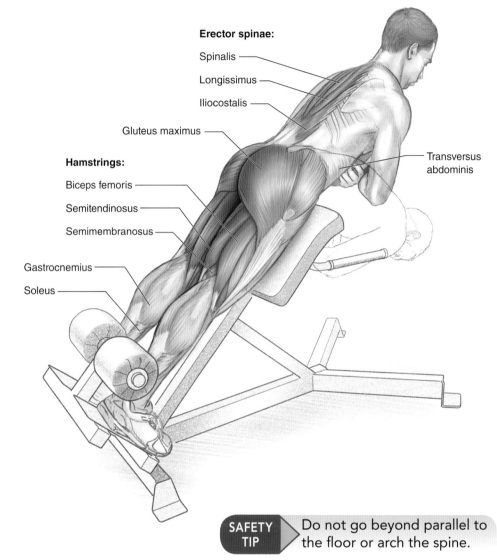

Erector spinae:

Spinalis

Longissimus

Iliocostalis

Gluteus maximus

Hamstrings:

Biceps femoris

Semitendinosus

Semimembranosus

Gastrocnemius

Soleus

Transversus abdominis

SAFETY TIP Do not go beyond parallel to the floor or arch the spine.

Execution

1. Using a hyperextension machine, position yourself prone and secure your feet under the foot pads with the fronts of your thighs resting on the main support pad. Your hips should be flexed forward at a 90-degree angle with your upper body hanging straight down. Keep your hands either behind your head or crossed in front of your body.

2. Slowly raise the trunk while maintaining a straight spine. All motion should occur at the hip. Rise until your torso is parallel to the floor and the angle of your hips is at 180 degrees. To make the exercise more demanding, pause for a second or two in the top position.

3. Lower your torso in a controlled manner until you reach the starting position.

4. Perform the prescribed number of repetitions.

Muscles Involved

Primary: Erector spinae (iliocostalis, longissimus, spinalis), gluteus maximus, hamstrings (biceps femoris, semimembranosus, semitendinosus)

Secondary: Transversospinalis, transversus abdominis, trapezius, rhomboids, gastrocnemius, soleus

Basketball Focus

The obvious implication for strengthening the posterior chain is to help with any jumping motion as well as to strengthen the muscles that maintain a good defensive posture of the upper body. Remember to keep your motion fluid, slow, and under control. Don't rock or swing your body. The hip acts as a hinge, and the upper torso remains stable. Do not go beyond parallel and excessively arch your spine because this can put unwanted stress on the vertebrae. Sometimes this exercise is called hyperextension, but that is a misnomer because it implies going into hyperextension when in fact you are coming from a flexed-forward position to a neutral-lumbar position.

⟨VARIATIONS⟩

Weighted Back Extension

To make this exercise more demanding, hold a weight plate or dumbbells against the chest for added resistance. Another way to add resistance is to secure elastic bands to the bottom of the hyperextension machine and loop them around the back of the neck and shoulders.

Machine-Free Back Extension

You can perform the back extension without a specific machine. Perform the same movement while lying prone over a Physioball with the feet secured against a wall or lie flat on your abdomen over a couple of pillows. Either option is a valid variation but may not allow for full motion the way a Roman chair or hyperextension machine allows.

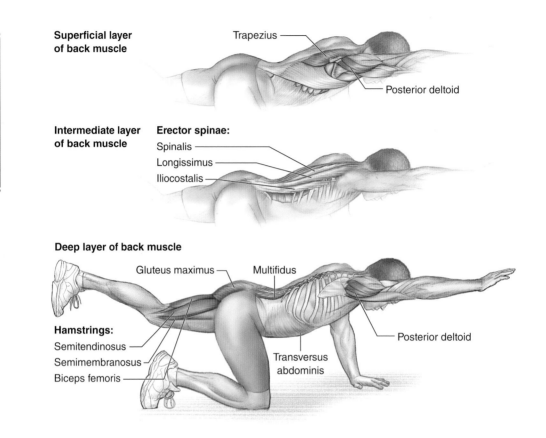

Superficial layer of back muscle — Trapezius — Posterior deltoid

Intermediate layer of back muscle — Erector spinae: Spinalis, Longissimus, Iliocostalis

Deep layer of back muscle — Gluteus maximus — Multifidus — Posterior deltoid

Hamstrings: Semitendinosus, Semimembranosus, Biceps femoris — Transversus abdominis

Execution

1. Assume an all-fours position on the floor with hips directly aligned over knees and shoulders over hands. Maintain a neutral spinal position. Draw in the abdominal muscles. Position the head and neck naturally with the eyes focused on the floor.

2. Lift one arm and the opposite leg straight out into full extension, achieving complete alignment with the torso. Do not allow either the hip or shoulder girdle to rotate. Maintain this extended position for the prescribed time, working on endurance of the muscles involved.

3. Return to the starting position and then lift the other arm and leg.

4. Repeat, alternating for the prescribed number of repetitions and sets.

Muscles Involved

Primary: Multifidus, transversus abdominis, gluteus maximus, hamstrings (biceps femoris, semimembranosus, semitendinosus), posterior deltoid, trapezius

Secondary: Erector spinae (iliocostalis, longissimus, spinalis), transversus abdominis

Basketball Focus

This is an excellent stability exercise for the core and spine. It helps develop torso strength so you can resist getting boxed out from under the basket. The ability to maintain your ground when defending or coming down from a rebound will enable you to dominate on the court. When lifting the arm and leg, imagine a carpenter's level left to right across the back of the shoulders and the hips. This will maintain spinal stability and resist the rotatory moment created by lifting opposite supports.

❮ VARIATION ❯

Weighted Bird Dog

To make this exercise more challenging, use cuff weights on the wrists and ankles or attach rubber tubing to opposing arm and leg pairs as added resistance.

HORIZONTAL CABLE CORE (PALLOF) PRESS

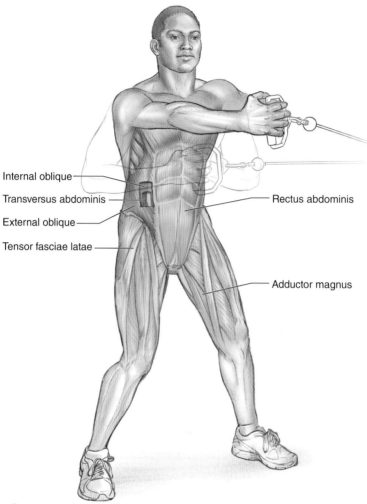

Internal oblique

Transversus abdominis

External oblique

Tensor fasciae latae

Rectus abdominis

Adductor magnus

Execution

1. Stand perpendicular to and directly in front of a cable column machine.

2. Assume an athletic stance with the feet shoulder-width apart and the knees slightly flexed, torso upright.

3. With both hands, grasp the handle attached to the cable column at middle level. Hold the handle close to the abdomen at about the height of the navel. Draw in the abdominal muscles and flex the buttocks.

4. While maintaining a straight torso, extend (press) the arms directly out in front of your body to shoulder height. This creates a greater rotational force that the hips and shoulders must resist. The purpose of this exercise is to resist this rotatory movement by maintaining a stable spinal position. Hold the extended press position for 1 to 5 seconds.

5. Return to the starting position. Perform 2 sets of 10 to 15 reps per side.

Muscles Involved

Primary: Multifidus, rotators, transversus abdominis, internal oblique, external oblique

Secondary: Rectus abdominis, erector spinae (iliocostalis, longissimus, spinalis), tensor fasciae latae, adductor magnus, gluteus maximus

Basketball Focus

This is an excellent antirotation exercise. The act of pressing is actually very easy, but resisting the rotational force makes this exercise taxing to the core muscles. It is critical to train your body to resist rotation as a way to protect the back. When you and another player are fighting for a rebound, the ability to hold the ball while an opponent is trying to strip the ball from you is crucial. Developing abdominal strength will help you defend and maintain possession of the ball.

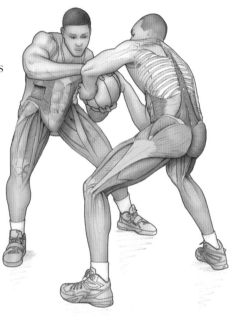

❮ VARIATION ❯

Tubing Pallof Press

This exercise is just as effective when performed with rubber tubing. Your coach may want to challenge you in a variety of stances and positions, such as a defensive position, to add a component of sport specificity or tall and half-kneeling positions to increase demand on core muscles. Making a narrower stance will increase the demand on the lower-extremity muscles as well.

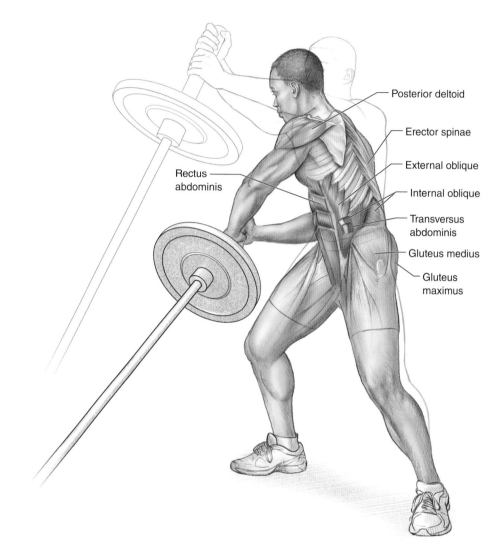

Posterior deltoid

Erector spinae

External oblique

Internal oblique

Transversus abdominis

Gluteus medius

Gluteus maximus

Rectus abdominis

Execution

1. Using an empty barbell with one end wedged securely in the corner of a wall, hold on to the other end with the arms extended in front of the body. Feet are just outside of shoulder width and shoulders and hips are squared off.

2. Using a rotating motion, twist the bar down and to the right in a smooth, semicircular pattern.

3. Once the bar comes to a complete stop at the bottom position, reverse the motion to the other side. The complete rotating motion is a 180-degree arc. There and back represents one full repetition. Perform 3 sets of 10 to 12 repetitions.

Muscles Involved

Primary: Rectus abdominis, transversus abdominis, internal oblique, external oblique

Secondary: Gluteus medius, gluteus maximus, erector spinae (iliocostalis, longissimus, spinalis), posterior deltoid

Basketball Focus

The landmine exercise is a compound exercise that uses a rotational movement. The trunk is responsible for the twisting motion occurring between the moving shoulder girdle and the stationary hip girdle. It is important to control the movement and not use momentum or a jerky motion. Improving rotational power and developing stronger trunk muscles will assist you when defending against an opponent. Rotational movements occur quickly when driving down the court or coming down from rebounding. You need strong core muscles to maintain stability and protect your back from injury.

⟨ VARIATION ⟩

Kneeling Landmine

You can perform this exercise from a kneeling or half-kneeling position. Performing this exercise in these positions eliminates the use of the muscles of the legs and hips.

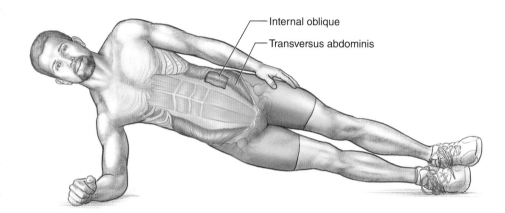

Internal oblique

Transversus abdominis

Execution

1. Lie on your left side with your feet, knees, hips, and shoulders in a straight line.
2. Prop your upper body on your left elbow and forearm. The elbow should be positioned directly under your shoulder.
3. Tighten your abdominal muscles as if you are bracing yourself to get punched in the stomach.
4. Raise your hips until they are in a straight line with your knees and shoulders.
5. Hold for the required time. Slowly lower your hips to the starting position.
6. Perform the prescribed number of repetitions. Repeat on the opposite side.

Muscles Involved

Primary: Transversus abdominis

Secondary: Internal oblique, multifidus, quadratus lumborum, longissimus thoracis

Basketball Focus

Lateral plank is probably the most effective exercise that you can perform anywhere to develop strong hips and trunk stability. Power is generated from the floor up. The ability to generate the most force into the floor can produce a higher jump and a faster run. When ascending for a jump shot or rebound, you need a strong core to stabilize the upper body and position yourself to make the next move. A strong core is the pillar of athletic movements. It allows you to withstand the rigors of banging bodies. The focus of this exercise is to improve your stability and balance when going up against bigger players.

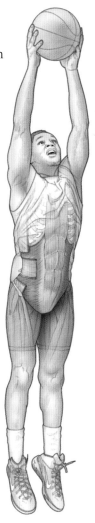

◀ VARIATION ▶

Modified Lateral Plank

If you are unable to maintain a straight line of the hips, knees, and shoulders, bend both knees and raise the hips.

OVERHEAD CABLE CORE PRESS

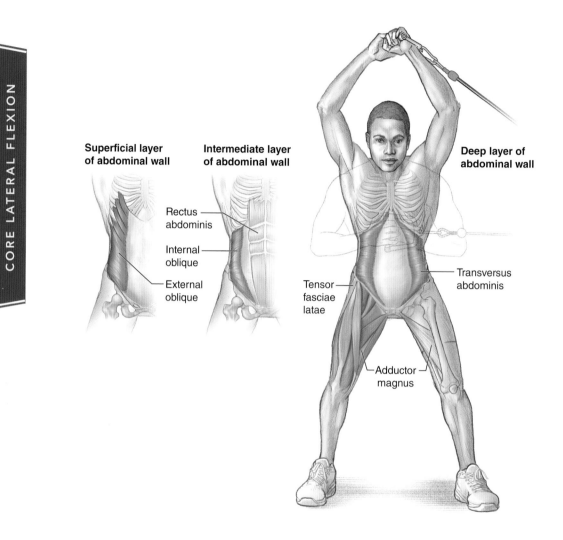

Superficial layer of abdominal wall

Intermediate layer of abdominal wall

Deep layer of abdominal wall

Rectus abdominis

Internal oblique

External oblique

Tensor fasciae latae

Transversus abdominis

Adductor magnus

Execution

1. Stand perpendicular to and directly in front of a cable column machine.

2. Assume an athletic stance with the feet shoulder-width apart, knees slightly flexed, and torso upright.

3. With both hands, grasp the handle attached to the cable column in the middle position. Hold the handle close to the abdomen at about the height of the navel. Draw in the abdominal muscles and flex the buttocks.

4. While maintaining a straight torso, extend (press) the arms directly overhead.

5. Return to the starting position and repeat for the prescribed number of repetitions.

Muscles Involved

Primary: Multifidus, rotators, transversus abdominis, internal oblique, external oblique

Secondary: Rectus abdominis, erector spinae (iliocostalis, longissimus, spinalis), tensor fasciae latae, adductor magnus, gluteus maximus

Basketball Focus

Not only does this exercise develop a stronger core, but it also develops shoulder stability during the overhead motion. This overhead motion develops the strength in the oblique muscles involved in lateral flexion. When you reach up for a rebound or shoot a three-pointer, you need this stability to ward off the defenders. This exercise develops strength in the shoulders and trunk when reaching up for a rebound. After jumping for a rebound or tipped ball, you might land in an awkward position. Developing the muscles to control lateral flexion can assist in preventing injuries to the low back and decrease the possibility of falling and causing other injuries.

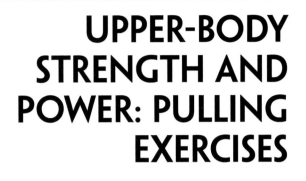
UPPER-BODY STRENGTH AND POWER: PULLING EXERCISES

ulling exercises are an important component in basketball training. Pulling-type exercises create a balance by complementing all of the pushing-type exercises performed during training. Pulling exercises also develop power in the shoulders, upper back, and arms. The posterior muscles involved with pulling exercises are the latissimus dorsi, trapezius, rhomboid major, rhomboid minor, teres major, teres minor, posterior deltoid, triceps brachii, supraspinatus, and infraspinatus. The anterior muscle groups involved in some pulling exercises are the brachialis, brachioradialis, anconeus, anterior deltoid, pectoralis major, pectoralis minor, and external obliques. These muscle groups are important in rebounding, shooting, offensive ball handling, establishing strategic offensive and defensive court position, and defending opponents. These exercises also help with grip strength in movements involving the barbell, dumbbell, and kettlebell. Grip strength is essential when controlling the basketball during ball handling, shooting, and rebounding activities.

Shoulder and back strength and power development enhance movement during competition. Running, cutting, and body control, especially when in the air, and injury prevention are important in basketball. Power enhancement will assist in more agile and higher velocity upper-body movements such as attempting to steal the basketball from an opponent.

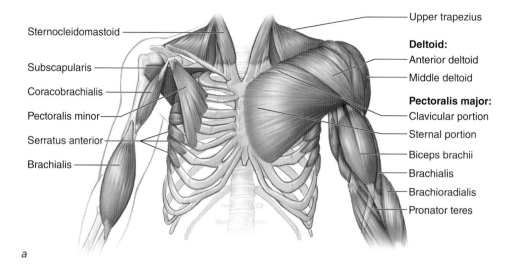

Sternocleidomastoid

Subscapularis

Coracobrachialis

Pectoralis minor

Serratus anterior

Brachialis

Upper trapezius

Deltoid:
Anterior deltoid
Middle deltoid

Pectoralis major:
Clavicular portion
Sternal portion
Biceps brachii
Brachialis
Brachioradialis
Pronator teres

a

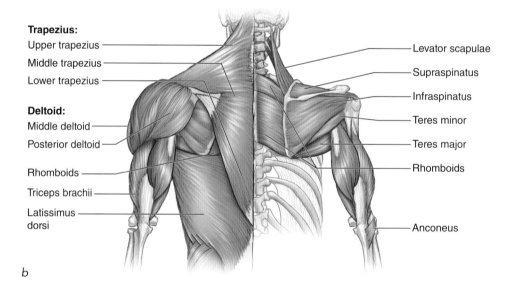

Trapezius:
Upper trapezius
Middle trapezius
Lower trapezius

Deltoid:
Middle deltoid
Posterior deltoid

Rhomboids

Triceps brachii

Latissimus dorsi

Levator scapulae

Supraspinatus

Infraspinatus

Teres minor

Teres major

Rhomboids

Anconeus

b

Figure 4.1   Upper torso: (a) anterior; (b) posterior.

This chapter covers the pulling exercises used for enhancing strength in the shoulders, upper back, and arms and power to assist you on the court.

Following are the exercises in this chapter:

Pull-up

Inverted row

Lat pull-down

Single-arm dumbbell row

Seated row

Barbell bent-over row

Kettlebell high pull

Renegade row

PULL-UP

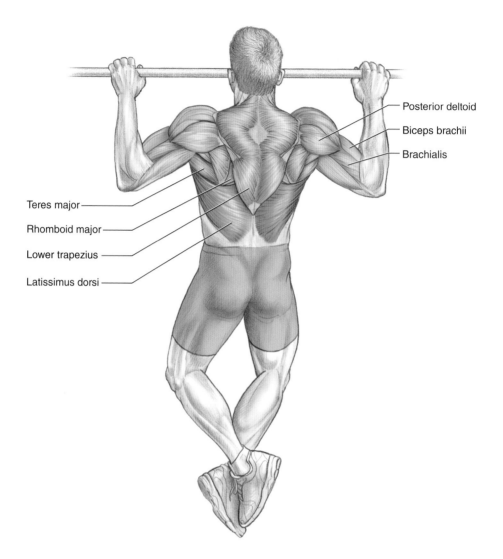

Posterior deltoid

Biceps brachii

Brachialis

Teres major

Rhomboid major

Lower trapezius

Latissimus dorsi

Execution

1. Hold the pull-up bar in an overhand grip, palms facing forward and arms fully extended with the body in a hanging position.

2. Slightly bend your knees and cross your ankles.

3. Start by pulling your body up, keeping your elbows in line with your body, until your chest is at the level of the bar.

4. Slowly lower back down until the arms are fully extended in the starting hanging position.

5. Perform the prescribed number of repetitions.

Muscles Involved

Primary: Latissimus dorsi

Secondary: Lower trapezius, rhomboid major, rhomboid minor, teres major, biceps brachii, brachialis

Basketball Focus

The pull-up is one of the most difficult exercises to execute, especially at the middle-school and high-school levels. The pull-up is easily varied: simply adjust your hand placement. When doing a wider grip pull-up, you will target the majority of the back muscles, but be cautious as this is the most advanced position for a pull-up. Beginners may want to use a narrow grip until they can perfect the pull-up. This will still develop the back muscles, but with some assistance from the secondary muscles. The pull-up exercise assists to develop all the necessary muscles in the upper back.

A strong back will assist the basketball athlete to be more effective when going up for a rebound or defending an opponent. Having a strong back will generate additional momentum when running down the court.

⟨VARIATIONS⟩

Band-Assisted Pull-Up

If you are unable to do a pull-up with body weight, try an assisted pull-up. Loop a heavy elastic band around the pull-up bar, making sure the band is secure around the bar. Place one or both knees into the loop of the band and perform the prescribed number of repetitions.

Different Hand Positions

- Grip the bar with the palms turned toward you to perform a chin-up.
- Grip the bar with one palm turned forward and one palm turned toward you (alternating grip).

INVERTED ROW

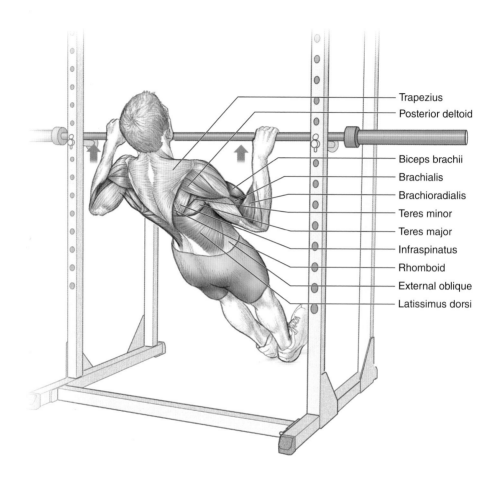

Trapezius
Posterior deltoid

Biceps brachii
Brachialis
Brachioradialis
Teres minor
Teres major
Infraspinatus
Rhomboid
External oblique
Latissimus dorsi

Execution

1. Adjust the height of a squat rack's safety supports so that while lying on the floor your arms are fully extended when you grip the bar.

2. Place a safely secured barbell on the supports in the squat rack.

3. Grip the bar with an overhand grip, palms turned forward, arms and legs fully extended.

4. Pull your body up toward the bar, making sure your hips and trunk rise at the same time.

5. End with your chest at the bar. Keep the elbows close to the body.

6. Lower back to the ground, making sure your hips and trunk stay in a straight line, until your arms are fully extended.

7. Perform the prescribed number of repetitions.

Muscles Involved

Primary: Latissimus dorsi, biceps brachii, brachialis, brachioradialis, posterior deltoid

Secondary: Rhomboid major, rhomboid minor, teres major, teres minor, infraspinatus, external oblique, trapezius

Basketball Focus

Similar to the pull-up, inverted rows help develop a strong back with an emphasis on the posterior deltoids. This exercise requires you to maintain a straight body position.

The inverted row helps you develop posterior shoulder strength, which can assist with long-range shooting ability and defending an opponent.

⟨VARIATIONS⟩

Tabletop Position

If you are unable to perform the exercise with the legs fully extended, bend the knees to 90 degrees and perform the prescribed number of repetitions.

TRX or Blast Straps

The exercise can be performed with TRX or blast straps. This will increase the difficulty of the exercise as the exercise performance requires that each arm be used independently to pull the body up.

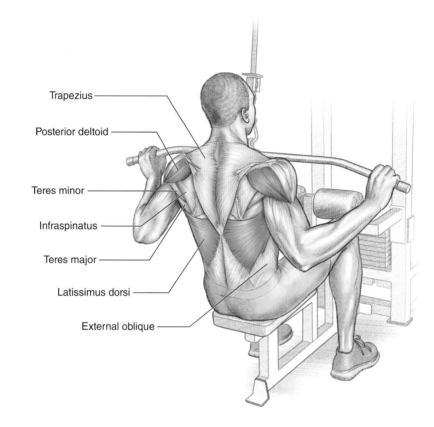

Trapezius

Posterior deltoid

Teres minor

Infraspinatus

Teres major

Latissimus dorsi

External oblique

Execution

1. Sit at a lat pull-down machine facing forward so the legs fit comfortably under the support pads.

2. Extend the arms overhead and grip the bar in an overhand grip, palms facing out. Place the hands a little wider than shoulder-width apart.

3. Lean back slightly. Initiate each repetition by pulling the bar toward your upper chest in a controlled motion until the bar touches the top of your chest. Keep your elbows close to the sides of your body.

4. Slowly return the bar to the starting position with your arms fully extended.

5. Perform the prescribed number of repetitions.

Muscles Involved

Primary: Latissimus dorsi, biceps brachii, brachialis, brachioradialis, posterior deltoid

Secondary: Rhomboid major, rhomboid minor, teres major, teres minor, infraspinatus, external oblique, trapezius

Basketball Focus

Similar in focus to pull-ups, the lat pull-down has the advantage of offering variable resistance for an athlete of various training experience to develop strength.

The lat pull-down will help to develop the pulling muscles of the upper back. The physical development of a strong back will assist with running and rebounding for a ball. Having strong back muscles will help with stabilization and control, which will help prevent injury. Basketball is becoming much more physical and players are becoming stronger. Because of the amount of contact that occurs under the basket, athletes need to become as strong as possible but still maintain their flexibility to shoot the ball. Having a well-developed back will assist in fending off an opponent who attempts to steal the ball.

‹VARIATIONS›

Close-Grip Lat Pull-Down

By bringing your grip closer toward the middle of the bar, you will work different muscle groups for your upper back. The close-grip lat pull-down focuses on the triceps brachii, rhomboid major, and rhomboid minor.

Reverse-Grip Lat Pull-Down

With a close grip, turn the hands so the palms face you. This will further incorporate the biceps brachii into the exercise performance.

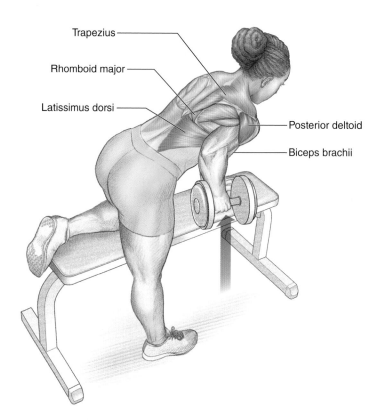

Trapezius

Rhomboid major

Latissimus dorsi

Posterior deltoid

Biceps brachii

Execution

1. From a standing position, flex your left knee to 90 degrees and place it on a bench.

2. Place your left hand on the bench to support your weight. Bend down to pick up a dumbbell with the right hand, letting the weight hang with the right arm extended.

3. Keeping your back flat and head in a neutral position, bring your hand up by flexing the elbow until your elbow is even with the side of your ribs.

4. Return the dumbbell to the starting position.

5. Perform the prescribed number of repetitions.

6. Switch sides and repeat the exercise with the left arm.

Muscles Involved

Primary: Posterior deltoid, latissimus dorsi

Secondary: Trapezius, rhomboid major, rhomboid minor, biceps brachii

Basketball Focus

The single-arm dumbbell row targets the posterior deltoids, an important muscle to develop for setting up a shot or rebounding. It is good at times to focus on single-limb movements to help develop the weakest link. When you perform an exercise that uses both arms or both legs, the more dominant side will tend to do most of the work. Incorporating single-arm dumbbell rows will help develop the weaker arm while maintaining the strength in the dominant arm. Having equal strength in both arms will benefit basketball players who are forced to shoot with their non-dominant hands.

‹ VARIATION ›

Single-Arm Band Row

Stand in a basketball defensive stance. Perform the one-arm rowing motion using a cable column or elastic band.

SEATED ROW

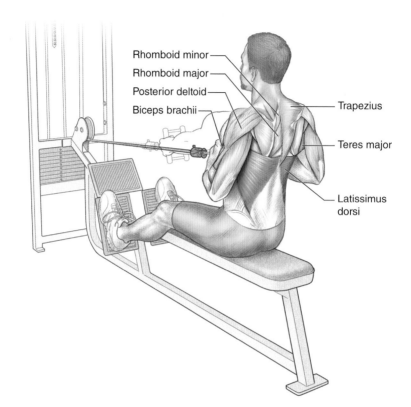

Rhomboid minor
Rhomboid major
Posterior deltoid
Biceps brachii
Trapezius
Teres major
Latissimus dorsi

Execution

1. Assume a seated position facing a cable column machine or use a seated row machine if one is available.

2. Place both feet securely on the platform with a slight bend in both knees.

3. Grasp the exercise handles with the palms facing each other to initiate the exercise movement.

4. Stabilizing the musculature of the upper back, pull the handles at a controlled speed toward your lower chest, while keeping your elbows to your sides.

5. Do not let elbows pass the sides of your body. Remember to keep your spine erect and do not lean back.

6. Maintaining a stable torso, return the handles to the starting position by extending the arms at a slow, controlled tempo.

7. Perform the prescribed number of repetitions.

Muscles Involved

Primary: Latissimus dorsi

Secondary: Trapezius, rhomboid major, rhomboid minor, teres major, posterior deltoid, biceps brachii

Basketball Focus

The upper back plays an important role in stabilizing the shoulder girdle and maintaining posture. Basketball players tend to have longer torsos, requiring stronger back muscles to help protect them from injuries that may occur when playing or driving to the hoop. As the game increases in contact under the boards and in the paint, basketball players need to have strength to fend off opponents and make openings with their bodies to score. The stronger, more powerful athlete will be able to accomplish this.

‹ VARIATION ›

Band Row

The rowing motion may also be performed from a standing position using elastic tubing or bands. This standing rowing motion also can be performed on a cable column using a straight bar.

Trapezius

Teres minor

Teres major

Biceps brachii

Posterior deltoid

Rhomboid major

Latissimus dorsi

Execution

1. Stand and hold a barbell in an overhand grip (palms facing the body), arms extended, and feet shoulder-width apart.

2. Hand position on the bar should be in line with or slightly wider than the shoulders.

3. Keeping the back flat, slightly bend the knees and lower the bar to just below your knees by shifting the hips back.

4. Pull the bar up in a straight line toward your lower chest, keeping the elbows close to the body. Squeeze the shoulder blades together.

5. Slowly lower the bar to the starting position while maintaining a flat back and bent knees.

6. Perform the prescribed number of repetitions.

Muscles Involved

Primary: Latissimus dorsi

Secondary: Trapezius, rhomboid major, rhomboid minor, teres major, posterior deltoid, biceps brachii

Basketball Focus

Although it has a similar focus as the seated row, the barbell bent-over row is a more advanced exercise. Performing this exercise in a standing position requires a strong low back and grip strength.

This exercise is essential in developing proper positioning for a solid athletic position. Strong back muscles are essential in basketball. You need strength in both the upper and lower back to handle the extensive running on the court, including quick bursts and sudden stops. The barbell bent-over row helps develop the upper back muscles.

‹VARIATIONS›

Grip Variation

You can perform the barbell bent-over row with a supinated grip (palms facing forward). This hand position will make it easier to keep the elbows close to the body during the exercise.

Dumbbell Bent-Over Row

If you are unable to perform a barbell bent-over row, perform the exercise with dumbbells and an adjustable bench. Adjust the bench to a 45-degree incline and straddle the bench, placing your chest on the incline portion of the bench while maintaining both feet flat on the floor. Holding the dumbbells in an overhand grip, bring the dumbbells to chest height and then slowly lower them to the starting position.

KETTLEBELL HIGH PULL

Trapezius

Teres minor

Lateral deltoid

Anterior deltoid

Starting position.

Execution

1. Stand erect with feet shoulder-width apart, toes turned slightly outward, and a kettlebell on the floor between your feet.

2. Squat while keeping the back flat and grasp the kettlebell in an overhand grip with both hands.

3. Holding the kettlebell with both arms extended, rise from the low-squat position, pushing through your heels, keeping the back flat.

4. Once the kettlebell reaches waist height, shrug the shoulders, thrust the hips forward, and flex the elbows explosively to pull the kettlebell to chest level.

5. The elbows should be parallel to the shoulders, back in an erect position, and heels off the floor.

6. Keeping the kettlebell close to the body, slowly lower the kettlebell back to the starting position by relaxing the shoulders, hips, and knees to return to the squat position until the kettlebell comes to rest on the floor between the feet.

7. Perform the prescribed number of repetitions.

Muscles Involved

Primary: Anterior deltoid, lateral deltoid

Secondary: Infraspinatus, supraspinatus, teres minor, trapezius

Basketball Focus

The kettlebell high pull is an excellent multijoint exercise that focuses on high-velocity movement that develops strong shoulders and explosive power for jumping and rebounding. You can do this exercise with either a kettlebell or a barbell. Moving the kettlebell or dumbbell at a high velocity will stimulate the nervous system and cause fast-twitch muscles to contract.

⟨ VARIATION ⟩

Barbell High Pull

You may also perform this exercise with a barbell. Start with the barbell in line with the tops of the shoelaces.

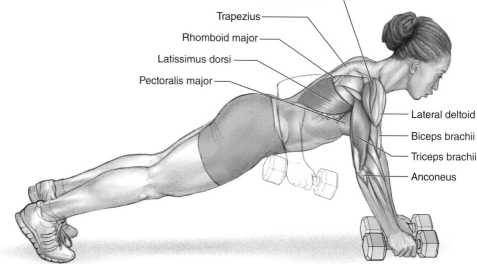

Posterior deltoid

Trapezius

Rhomboid major

Latissimus dorsi

Pectoralis major

Lateral deltoid

Biceps brachii

Triceps brachii

Anconeus

Execution

1. Assume a push-up position with the hands grasping the handles of a pair of dumbbells. The arms should be extended with both feet firmly placed on the ground. The back should be flat and in line with the hips, shoulders, and legs.

2. While stabilizing the left arm on the dumbbell, perform a single-arm row with the right arm. Raise the dumbbell to just below the chest, keeping the elbow close to the body. Keep the shoulders, hips, and legs in line and avoid rotating during the exercise.

3. Return the dumbbell to the starting position. Execute the same motion with the other arm.

4. Perform the prescribed number of repetitions for each arm.

Muscles Involved

Primary: Triceps brachii, pectoralis major, posterior deltoid, latissimus dorsi

Secondary: Pectoralis minor, anterior deltoid, anconeus, trapezius, rhomboid major, rhomboid minor, biceps brachii

Basketball Focus

Developing a stronger upper body allows you to pass and receive the ball more quickly. Upper-body strength allows for improved balance and posture when rebounding or shooting. The strength gained from this exercise will protect your shoulders and prevent injury. The renegade row incorporates pushing and pulling motions to target the pectoralis major, pectoralis minor, and anterior deltoid during the pushing motion and strengthen the rhomboid major and rhomboid minor during the pulling motion.

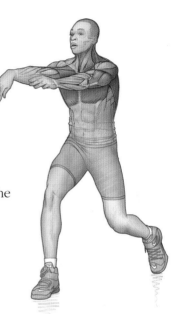

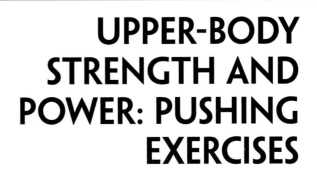

UPPER-BODY STRENGTH AND POWER: PUSHING EXERCISES

s stated in chapter 1, basketball and many other athletic endeavors are played from the ground up, and the upper extremity is the last link in the body's kinetic chain to receive the forces produced. When you perform a jump shot, the forces are initiated from the floor via the legs and transmitted through the body via the core to conclude at the upper extremities with the ball release.

The upper body also has a direct relationship to running velocity. Try this experiment: Sit on the floor with the legs fully extended and the torso in an upright position. Pump the arms forward and backward, mimicking the arm motion that occurs with running. Start moving the arms slowly as you would while jogging and build up the arm speed to move quickly as in sprinting. You will notice during the very high arm speeds that the hips and legs begin to move back and forth, contributing to the execution.

The upper body is important in basketball. The game requires you to be very physical when guarding an opponent, positioning for a rebound, passing the ball, attacking a defensive opponent, and going up strong to score from under the basket. Since much of the sport is played overhead (shooting, rebounding, and so on), upper-body strength and power are required for sustaining optimal performance throughout the season and preventing injuries to the upper extremities.

When designing an upper-body strength and power program, incorporate both agonist and antagonist muscle groups to maintain an appropriate balance of the upper-body musculature so that the goals of optimal performance and the prevention of upper-body injury are established.

The long basketball season of practices and competitions is physically taxing on your body. Research has demonstrated that upper-body fatigue and, more specifically, fatigue in the shoulder muscles, have a negative effect on shoulder joint kinematics and may set the table for possible injury as the season progresses. Effective upper-body strength and power training will establish a platform of resistance to assist in the prevention of injury.

In this chapter we discuss some of the strength and power exercises that enhance the upper-body and optimize performance on the court. We focus on the pectoralis major and pectoralis minor (figure 5.1*a*), which are used for pushing motions, such as in the bench press and push-up. These muscles help you be more explosive when passing the ball. Overhead exercises use the deltoids and stabilizing muscles such as the latissimus dorsi and supraspinatus (figure 5.1*b*).

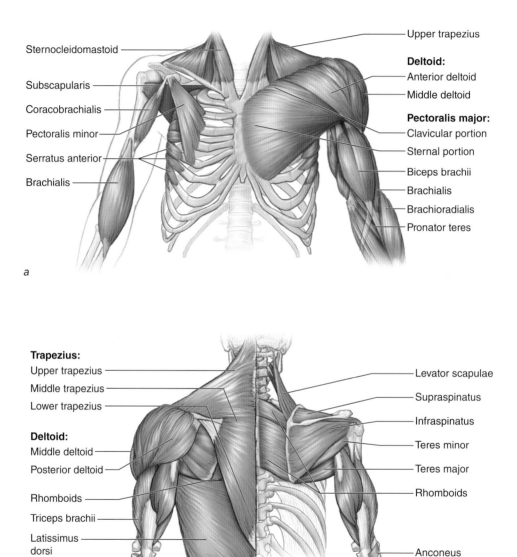

Sternocleidomastoid

Subscapularis

Coracobrachialis

Pectoralis minor

Serratus anterior

Brachialis

Upper trapezius

Deltoid:
Anterior deltoid
Middle deltoid

Pectoralis major:
Clavicular portion
Sternal portion

Biceps brachii
Brachialis
Brachioradialis
Pronator teres

a

Trapezius:
Upper trapezius
Middle trapezius
Lower trapezius

Deltoid:
Middle deltoid
Posterior deltoid

Rhomboids
Triceps brachii
Latissimus dorsi

Levator scapulae
Supraspinatus
Infraspinatus
Teres minor
Teres major
Rhomboids

Anconeus

b

Figure 5.1   Muscles of the upper torso: (*a*) anterior; (*b*) posterior.

Following are the exercises in this chapter:

Push-up
Bench press
Overhead press
Single-arm band press
Incline barbell press
Single-arm landmine press
Close-grip bench press

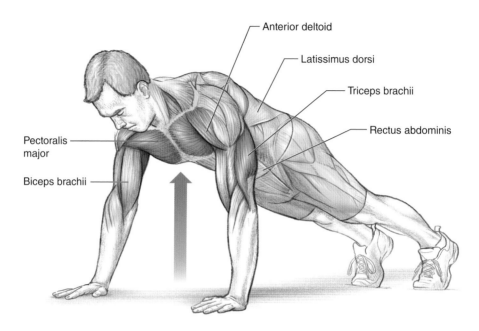
PUSH-UP

Anterior deltoid

Latissimus dorsi

Triceps brachii

Rectus abdominis

Pectoralis major

Biceps brachii

Execution

1. Lie on your belly. Place your hands slightly wider than shoulder width, fingers pointing forward, and thumbs in line with the top of the chest. The elbows are close to the torso.

2. Maintaining a flat back and engaging the abdominal muscles, press the palms of the hands into the floor, moving the body away from the floor by extending the arms. The hips and shoulders must rise simultaneously.

3. Slowly lower yourself to the starting position, maintaining hip and shoulder position and controlling the descent.

4. Perform the prescribed number of repetitions.

Muscles Involved

Primary: Pectoralis major, triceps brachii, anterior deltoid

Secondary: Biceps brachii, latissimus dorsi, rectus abdominis

Basketball Focus

The push-up is all athletes' building block for moving the body weight in a controlled motion. The push-up targets key muscles in the torso and upper arms, which are important during basketball. The ability to chest-pass the ball explosively can give your team an edge in setting up a strong offensive drive. The horizontal movement used to pass a basketball is seen in many barbell and dumbbell exercises. A stronger upper body also helps when defending an opponent or setting a pick for a teammate.

‹VARIATIONS›

Knee Push-Up

Beginners and weaker athletes initially can perform the push-up on the knees until upper-body strength improves.

Platform Push-Up

Advanced athletes can perform the push-up with the feet placed on a 12- to 24-inch (30-60 cm) platform.

◀ BENCH PRESS ▶

Anterior deltoid

Triceps brachii

Pectoralis major

 SAFETY TIP Always have a spotter present when performing the bench press.

Execution

1. Lie on your back on a flat weight bench with the knees bent at a 90-degree angle and both feet flat on the floor.

2. Hold a barbell slightly wider than shoulder width, wrapping the thumbs around the bar.

3. Remove the barbell from the bench by retracting (pinching) the scapula to create a platform from which to push.

4. Fully extend the arms.

5. Slowly lower the barbell, controlling the descent, by bending your elbows while maintaining the upper arms at a 45-degree angle to the body.

6. Continue to lower the bar until it touches at approximately midchest (nipple level). Do not bounce the bar off your chest.

7. Under a slow, controlled exhalation, push the bar away from your chest. Keep your low back flat on the bench and maintain a 45-degree upper-arm angle. Extend the arms to the starting position.

8. Perform the prescribed number of repetitions.

Muscles Involved

Primary: Pectoralis major, pectoralis minor

Secondary: Anterior deltoid, triceps brachii

Basketball Focus

Similar to the push-up, the bench press is the next progression in developing upper-body strength. You must use proper form and spotting techniques to prevent any serious injuries. This exercise engages and strengthens the muscles of the chest, anterior shoulder, and triceps. A stronger upper body will help you absorb some of the pounding that can occur under the basket.

◄ VARIATION ►

Dumbbell Bench Press

Perform the bench press using dumbbells.

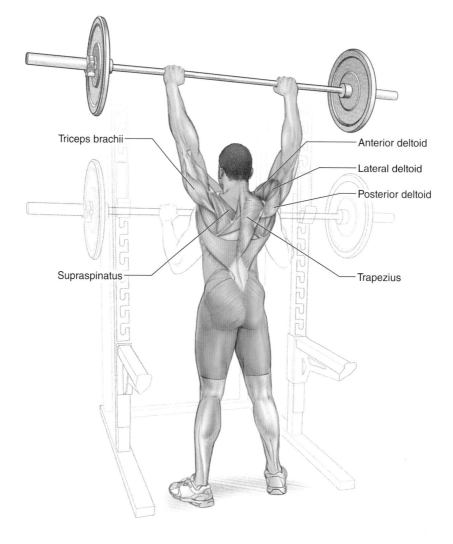

Triceps brachii

Anterior deltoid

Lateral deltoid

Posterior deltoid

Supraspinatus

Trapezius

 SAFETY TIP When pressing the barbell overhead, do not arch or overextend the lower back.

Execution

1. Stand in a squat rack with a barbell at approximately upper-chest height.
2. Walk into the rack until your upper chest touches the bar.
3. Grip the barbell with hands slightly wider than shoulder width and thumbs wrapped around the bar.

4. Lift the bar slightly off the rack and place it on the upper chest and anterior deltoids.

5. Take one or two steps back, positioning your feet slightly wider than shoulder width.

6. While maintaining an erect posture, take a deep inhalation and use slow and controlled exhalation (as in the bench press) as you push the barbell overhead by fully extending your arms. The barbell should travel directly over your head, concluding with the arms fully extended and in line with both ears.

7. Slowly lower the barbell to your upper chest, controlling the descent and maintaining an erect posture.

8. Perform the prescribed number of repetitions.

Muscles Involved

Primary: Anterior deltoid, lateral deltoid, supraspinatus

Secondary: Pectoralis major, posterior deltoid, trapezius, supraspinatus, triceps brachii

Basketball Focus

Many athletes are weakest in overhead exercises. As with the bench press, proper form is required for preventing injury. When done correctly, the overhead press engages the muscles of the anterior deltoid, lateral deltoid, supraspinatus, and triceps brachii. Since this exercise is done in a standing position, the rectus abdominis and back extensor muscles must be activated to stabilize the torso. The overhead press enhances upper-body and shoulder strength, which are required for shooting and rebounding.

< VARIATION >

Seated Dumbbell Overhead Press
You may perform this exercise while seated and with dumbbells for variety.

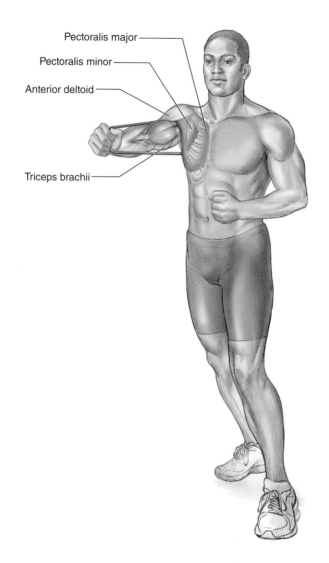

Pectoralis major

Pectoralis minor

Anterior deltoid

Triceps brachii

Execution

1. Attach an exercise band tightly to a secure object. Loop the band so it fits in the palm of the right hand.

2. Turn 180 degrees and face the opposite direction from where the band is secured. Walk forward until you achieve the desired tension in the band.

3. Assume a staggered stance with the left leg in front of the right leg.

4. Flex the right elbow to 90 degrees, maintaining an arm position next to the body.

5. Maintaining a solid posture and stance, push the band forward by extending the elbow and shoulder straight ahead, simulating a pressing motion. Keep the band at shoulder height and maintain control of the band.

6. In a slow, controlled manner, return the arm to the starting position.

7. Repeat with the band in the left hand and the right foot forward in the staggered stance.

8. Perform the prescribed number of repetitions.

Muscles Involved

Primary: Pectoralis major, pectoralis minor

Secondary: Anterior deltoid, triceps brachii

Basketball Focus

If you do not have access to a gym or weights, a good investment is elastic band or tubing that has adequate resistance. This variation of the single-arm press will benefit the weaker nondominant side by developing the pectoralis major, pectoralis minor, and anterior deltoid. Since you are in a staggered stance, this exercise engages the muscles that stabilize the torso. This exercise develops shoulder strength for passing and dribbling. You also need upper-body strength if you encounter a defender blocking your path to the basket.

Pectoralis major

Pectoralis minor

Anterior deltoid   Triceps brachii

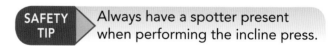

SAFETY TIP   Always have a spotter present when performing the incline press.

Execution

1. Sit on an incline bench or an adjustable bench set at a 45-degree angle. Your back, shoulders, and head are in contact with the bench.

2. Place both feet firmly on the floor. Hold the barbell in a grip slightly wider than shoulder width, thumbs wrapped around the bar.

3. Retract the scapula to establish a platform from which to push.

4. Lift the bar by extending the arms until the bar is at approximately eye level.

5. Slowly lower the barbell, controlling the descent, by bending your elbows. Keep your upper arms at a 45-degree angle to your body until the barbell touches the upper chest. Be sure not to bounce the bar off your chest.

6. With a controlled exhalation, push the bar away from your chest. Keep your lower back flat on the bench as you extend the arms to the starting position.

7. Perform the prescribed number of repetitions.

Muscles Involved

Primary: Pectoralis major, pectoralis minor, anterior deltoid

Secondary: Lateral deltoid, triceps brachii

Basketball Focus

This exercise is similar to the bench press for developing upper-body strength. The incline position targets the pectoralis muscle groups (mostly the upper chest) and places more emphasis on the anterior deltoid and triceps than the flat bench press does. The angle of the incline can vary based on equipment used. The standard incline is usually 45 degrees, but some athletes may prefer 60 degrees, based on comfort level. Upper-body strength helps you exert more force when performing a chest pass and to maintain position when underneath the boards.

‹VARIATION›

Incline Dumbbell Press

You may perform this exercise using dumbbells.

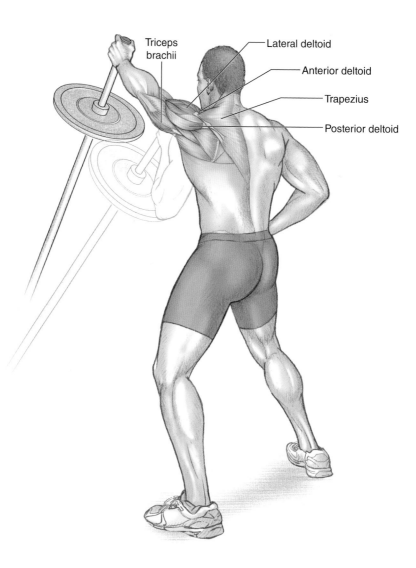

Triceps brachii

Lateral deltoid

Anterior deltoid

Trapezius

Posterior deltoid

Execution

1. Place one end of a barbell in a landmine apparatus. If a landmine apparatus is unavailable, place one end of a barbell into the bottom corner of a wall.

2. Place an appropriate weight plate at the opposite end of the barbell.

3. Standing with the hips and knees flexed in a good defensive stance, grab the weighted end of the bar with the left hand and lift the bar up, rotating the elbow forward so the bar is resting in the palm at shoulder height. Maintain an elbow position close to your body.

4. Maintaining your solid defensive stance, extend the arm holding the barbell up and forward until the arm is fully extended.

5. Slowly lower the barbell to the starting position. Perform the prescribed number of repetitions.

6. Repeat the exercise using the right arm.

Muscles Involved

Primary: Anterior deltoid, lateral deltoid, supraspinatus

Secondary: Pectoralis major, posterior deltoid, trapezius, triceps brachii

Basketball Focus

This is not a traditional single-arm exercise, but it is an alternative for developing shoulder strength. The single-arm landmine press is beneficial in developing anterior and lateral deltoid muscles. Using a single-arm action also develops stability in the shoulder and trunk.

This exercise mimics the overhead position as seen in a layup or dunk. Stronger shoulders will help when you go up for a rebound.

⟨VARIATIONS⟩

Double-Arm Landmine Press
You may perform this exercise with two hands on the bar.

Staggered-Stance Landmine Press
You may perform this exercise while in a staggered stance.

CLOSE-GRIP BENCH PRESS

Anconeus   Triceps   Pectoralis
            brachii   major

SAFETY TIP ▷ A spotter should be present during the exercise.

Execution

1. Lie flat on a weight bench with knees bent at a 90-degree angle, feet flat on the floor.

2. Place the hands less than shoulder-width apart (closer to midchest region) and grip the barbell with your thumbs around the bar.

3. Retract your scapula to establish a platform from which to push. Extend the arms to lift the barbell to approximately eye level.

4. Slowly lower the barbell, controlling the descent, by bending your elbows and keeping the upper arm at a 45-degree angle to the body. The barbell should descend to touch at the midchest (nipple) level. Be sure not to bounce the bar off your chest.

5. With a slow, controlled exhalation, push the bar away from your chest. Keep your lower back flat on the bench.

6. Extend the arms while maintaining the 45-degree upper-arm position as you return to the starting position.

7. Perform the prescribed number of repetitions.

Muscles Involved

Primary: Triceps brachii, pectoralis major

Secondary: Pectoralis minor, anterior deltoid, anconeus

Basketball Focus

The close-grip bench press is similar to the flat bench press, but more focus is on the triceps brachii and pectoralis major. Close-grip bench pressing helps you develop strength to position yourself to block a shot or fend off an opponent who is trying to steal the ball. This exercise builds strength in the upper body so that you become stronger and more explosive when performing a chest pass.

chapter 6

EXPLOSIVE WEIGHT TRAINING FOR PLAYING ABOVE THE RIM

Explosive weight training is synonymous with the ability to produce power. The quality of work relates to producing a force that causes a displacement. This would occur as a muscle produces force to lift a weight over a specified distance. Work has nothing to do with the duration in which muscular forces act to cause the displacement. Strength is expressed in this formula:

$$\text{work} = \text{force} \times \text{distance}$$

When lifting heavy weights such as in the squat, deadlift, and bench press, these strength movements do not require an element of time for you to conclude the repetition. Power, on the other hand, does have a factor of time to conclude the repetition. The formula for power is as follows:

$$\text{power} = (\text{force} \times \text{distance}) / \text{time}$$

Therefore, when you weight train with the intention of developing explosive power, you would perform these types of exercises in a very short time. Although two different exercises may involve the same amount of work, the exercise executed in the shortest time (performed at the highest velocity) would elicit the most power. The ability to produce force very quickly also occurs at the highest rate of force development (RFD). The RFD of a muscle is the maximal rate of rise in the force generated during the early phase of a muscle contraction. The RFD is imperative for success in sports. Most athletic skills are performed in a brief time (200 to 300 ms); the time to produce maximum muscular force may take up to 500 milliseconds. Therefore, the strongest athlete on the team may not always be as effective as the most powerful athlete on the team (see figure 6.1). For example, since there is limited time to accelerate past or jump higher than an opponent, an athlete who can produce muscular force quickly will have an advantage over an opponent who may be stronger but is slower in producing muscular force.

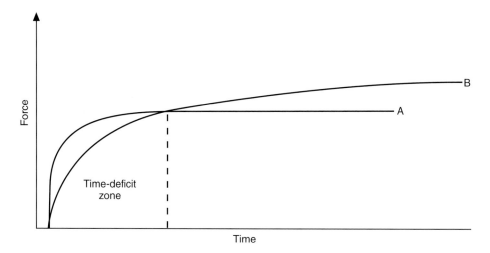

Figure 6.1   Force-time histories of two athletes, A and B. In the time-deficit zone, athlete A is stronger than athlete B.

Reprinted, by permission, from V.M. Zatsiorsky and W.J. Kraemer, 2006, *Science and practice of strength training*, 2nd ed. (Champaign, IL: Human Kinetics), 28.

Continued gains in the physical quality of strength are not always beneficial for athletic performance and, at a certain time in the training program, the training emphasis should shift from strength to power for optimal performance. You must ensure that you've established a strong strength base before emphasizing power-type activities.

This chapter discusses exercises that enhance the ability to produce force in a brief duration, thus enhancing power. Note that with all of the exercises described in this chapter, the vertical displacement of the barbell occurs as the result of efforts of the legs and hips, not by pulling on the barbell with the arms.

Following are the exercises in this chapter:

Kettlebell swing
Snatch pull from hang position
Clean pull from hang position
Power snatch from hang position
Power snatch from floor
Power clean from hang position

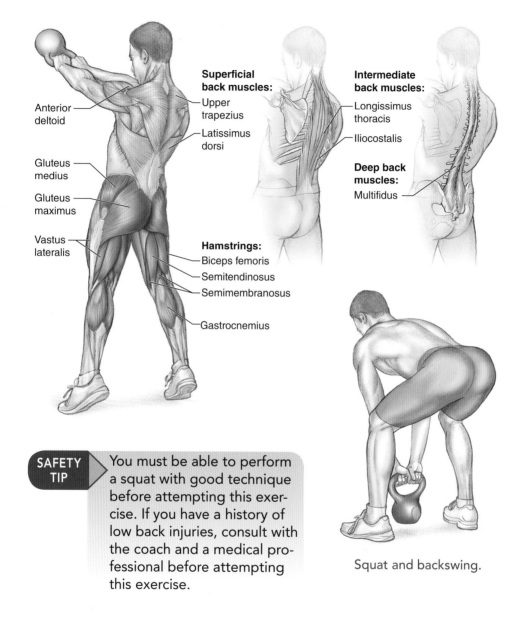

Anterior deltoid

Gluteus medius

Gluteus maximus

Vastus lateralis

Superficial back muscles:
Upper trapezius

Latissimus dorsi

Hamstrings:
Biceps femoris

Semitendinosus

Semimembranosus

Gastrocnemius

Intermediate back muscles:
Longissimus thoracis

Iliocostalis

Deep back muscles:
Multifidus

Squat and backswing.

SAFETY TIP You must be able to perform a squat with good technique before attempting this exercise. If you have a history of low back injuries, consult with the coach and a medical professional before attempting this exercise.

Execution

1. Stand upright, holding a kettlebell with both hands, arms relaxed in front of the body with the kettlebell between your legs. Assume a wide stance with the feet outside shoulder width and toes pointing slightly out.

2. Squat while keeping the back straight and your eyes and head facing forward. Push the hips back as you descend until the kettlebell is well clear of your groin between your legs.

3. To initiate the swing, press your forearms against your groin as the kettlebell extends behind you. Once the kettlebell has reached its farthest point between your legs, immediately extend the hips upward and thrust them forward. This will cause the back to straighten vertically and the kettlebell to move forward in an upward arc.

4. As the kettlebell moves forward, fully extend the arms until the kettlebell rises to chest height. Do not use your arms to move the kettlebell. Momentum from your hips and legs should initiate all movement.

5. Once the kettlebell reaches optimal chest height, let the kettlebell lower into its arc of motion as you squat down slightly, keeping the hips back and your back in a neutral position.

6. Perform the prescribed number of repetitions.

Muscles Involved

Primary: Gluteus maximus, gluteus medius, hamstrings (semitendinosus, biceps femoris, semimembranosus), quadriceps (rectus femoris, vastus lateralis, vastus medialis, vastus intermedius), gastrocnemius

Secondary: Anterior deltoid, multifidus, longissimus thoracis, iliocostalis, latissimus dorsi, upper trapezius

Basketball Focus

The kettlebell swing is a good introductory exercise for teaching athletes hip thrusting and the triple extension movement pattern (extend at the ankles, knees, and hips) to assist with the teaching progression of Olympic-type weightlifting exercises. The triple extension is an important component of running and jumping. This exercise teaches you to produce higher forces into the floor when running after an opponent or when jumping for a rebound. Good explosiveness on the court enables you to move more quickly and outjump an opponent.

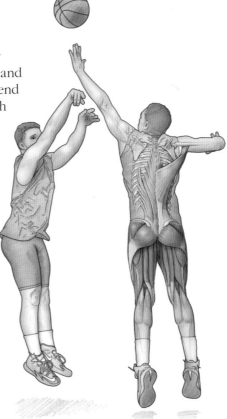

SNATCH PULL FROM HANG POSITION

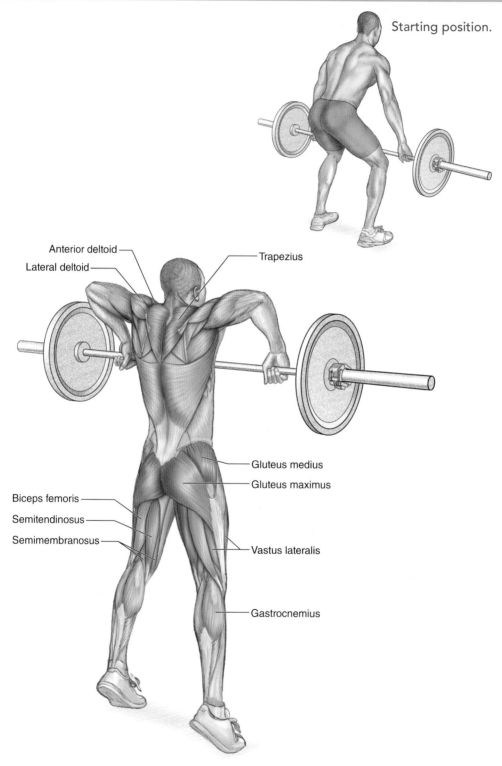

Starting position.

Anterior deltoid

Lateral deltoid

Trapezius

Gluteus medius

Gluteus maximus

Biceps femoris

Semitendinosus

Semimembranosus

Vastus lateralis

Gastrocnemius

Execution

1. Grip the barbell with the hands significantly wider than the shoulders. Place the barbell against the midthighs, just above the knees. The shoulders should be slightly over (in front of) the barbell with knees slightly bent, back flat, and head facing straight ahead.

2. Initiate pulling the barbell up by extending the legs while simultaneously thrusting the hips forward and bending the elbows as the barbell rises toward the shoulders. Keep the barbell close to the body, and do not allow it to swing away during this process.

3. The barbell should rise to approximately chest level as the ankles, knees, and hips fully extend at the maximum height of the bar.

4. Once you achieve maximum bar height, slowly decelerate and lower the bar to the starting position by flexing the knees and sitting back with the hips.

5. Perform the prescribed number of repetitions.

Muscles Involved

Primary: Gluteus maximus, gluteus medius, semitendinosus, vastus lateralis, vastus medialis, vastus intermedius, trapezius, lateral deltoid, anterior deltoid

Secondary: Gastrocnemius, biceps femoris, semimembranosus, rectus femoris

Basketball Focus

The snatch pull is a good exercise to learn before initiating the snatch exercise. As with any other skill, practice and technique are important components to perfecting this exercise. The force produced when performing the snatch pull can improve jumping abilities. This quick and explosive activity will also prepare you to be more explosive on the court.

CLEAN PULL FROM HANG POSITION

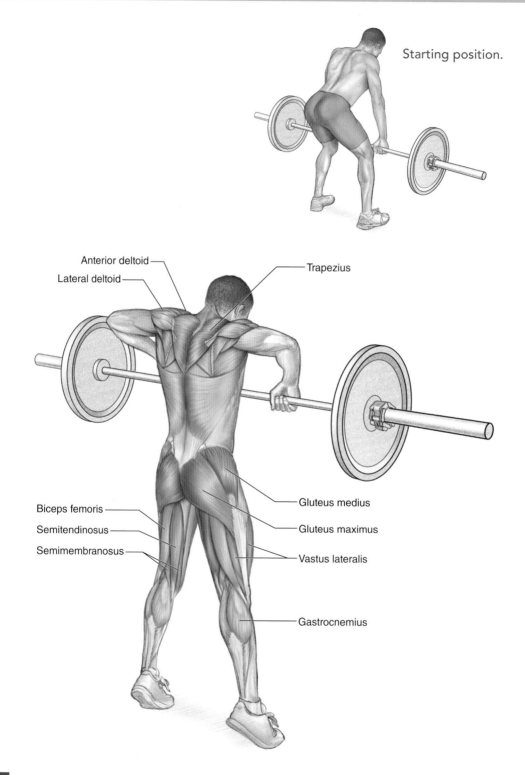

Starting position.

Anterior deltoid

Lateral deltoid

Trapezius

Biceps femoris

Semitendinosus

Semimembranosus

Gluteus medius

Gluteus maximus

Vastus lateralis

Gastrocnemius

Execution

1. Grip the barbell with the hands just outside of the knees. Position the barbell against the midthighs, just above the knees, with the shoulders slightly over (in front of) the barbell, knees slightly bent, back flat, and head facing straight ahead.

2. Raise the barbell by extending the hips and legs, keeping the bar close to the body while bending the elbows as the bar rises.

3. The barbell should rise to chest level or slightly below as the ankles, knees, and hips are fully extended at the maximum height of the bar.

4. Once you achieve maximum bar height, slowly decelerate and lower the bar to the starting position by flexing the knees and sitting back with the hips.

5. Perform the prescribed number of repetitions.

Muscles Involved

Primary: Gluteus maximus, gluteus medius, semitendinosus, vastus lateralis, vastus medialis, vastus intermedius, trapezius, lateral deltoid, anterior deltoid

Secondary: Gastrocnemius, biceps femoris, semimembranosus, rectus femoris

Basketball Focus

Similar to the snatch pull exercise, the clean pull is a good exercise to perform before the initiation of the clean exercise. Although the exercises are similar, the variation of the grip and weight intensity allows a training variation that will help develop a positive training adaptation. Just as with any other skill, practice and technique are important components in perfecting this exercise. The clean pull teaches you how to develop force into the floor and be more explosive, which are required for jumping and accelerating.

Anterior deltoid
Lateral deltoid
Trapezius

Biceps femoris
Semitendinosus
Semimembranosus

Gluteus medius
Gluteus maximus
Vastus lateralis
Gastrocnemius

Bar slightly above knees.

Triple extension and shoulder shrug.

Execution

1. Approach the barbell and grasp the bar with the hands significantly wider than the shoulders. Place the barbell against the midthighs, just above the knees.

2. After picking up the bar, assume an erect standing position with the knees slightly bent.

3. Moving the hips back but not changing the knee angle, lower the bar to a position slightly above the knees.

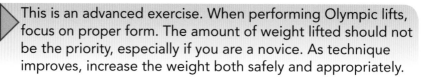

SAFETY TIP This is an advanced exercise. When performing Olympic lifts, focus on proper form. The amount of weight lifted should not be the priority, especially if you are a novice. As technique improves, increase the weight both safely and appropriately.

EXPLOSIVE MOVEMENTS

4. The chest should be over and in front of the barbell. The upper back is straight and the lower back is in a neutral position. The arms are relaxed and completely straight.

5. Quickly extend the lower extremities as the hips move forward, continuing to maintain the knee bend because this will cause the barbell to slide up the front of the legs.

6. Fully extend the knees and ankles and quickly shrug the shoulders, causing the barbell to rise vertically.

7. Once the barbell has reached its highest point, slightly drop by bending the knees. Conclude the exercise by extending the arms to receive the barbell as it travels over and slightly behind the head.

8. Perform the prescribed number of repetitions.

Muscles Involved

Primary: Gluteus maximus, gluteus medius, semitendinosus, vastus lateralis, vastus medialis, vastus intermedius, trapezius, lateral deltoid, anterior deltoid

Secondary: Gastrocnemius, biceps femoris, semimembranosus, rectus femoris

Basketball Focus

The power snatch from hang position is an advanced exercise. To master form and generate a fast and correct barbell pathway, use light weights or an unweighted barbell when initially performing this exercise. This exercise develops explosive power and total-body strength. As the bar rises overhead, it aids in shoulder stability and core strength because you have to stabilize the weight overhead. Shoulder stability and core strength are important for maintaining posture when off the floor. The explosive movement of the snatch simulates the movement of jump shots and rebounds.

⟨ VARIATION ⟩

Power Snatch From Box

Before starting, place the barbell on boxes of various heights (3-12 in., or 6 to 30 cm). Box height can be adjusted based on the desired position of the barbell. Boxes may be stacked on each other to adjust the barbell position above the knee, at the knee, or below the knee. Starting exercises from various box heights will teach you to explode from a dead stop.

Starting position.

Anterior deltoid
Lateral deltoid
Trapezius

Gluteus medius
Gluteus maximus
Rectus femoris
Semitendinosus
Semimembranosus
Vastus lateralis
Biceps femoris
Gastrocnemius

Execution

1. Approach the barbell and grasp the bar with the hands significantly wider than the shoulders.
2. Lift the bar off the floor by raising the hips and shoulders simultaneously. The barbell stays close to the body until it is just above the knees.
3. The chest is over and in front of the barbell. The upper back is straight and the lower back is neutral. The arms are relaxed and completely straight.
4. Quickly extend the lower limbs as the hips move forward. Maintain the knee bend as the barbell slides up the front of the legs.
5. Fully extend the knees and ankles as you quickly shrug the shoulders, causing the barbell to rise vertically.
6. Once the barbell has reached its highest point, slightly drop by bending the knees. Conclude the exercise by extending the arms to receive the barbell as it travels over and slightly behind the head.
7. Perform the prescribed number of repetitions

Muscles Involved

Primary: Gluteus maximus, gluteus medius, semitendinosus, vastus lateralis, vastus medialis, vastus intermedius, trapezius, lateral deltoid, anterior deltoid

Secondary: Gastrocnemius, biceps femoris, semimembranosus, rectus femoris

Basketball Focus

Starting with the bar on the floor is the most advanced variation of the power snatch. This position may be difficult for taller athletes because it requires great joint mobility and muscle flexibility to maintain the starting position posture. If you can assume this starting exercise position, your hips and shoulders must rise simultaneously to start the first pull of the exercise performance. As you begin to rise, the barbell should stay close to the body until the barbell is above the knees.

Lifting weights from the floor will assist you in your ability to accelerate. Think of this like a NASCAR racer. As the driver moves around the track, he accelerates when he needs to pass an opponent. Thus, there is a preparatory movement (moving around the race track) before the moment of acceleration. When lifting the barbell from the floor, a slow preparatory movement of pulling the bar to the height of the knees occurs before the explosive acceleratory movement that occurs when the barbell reaches the knees.

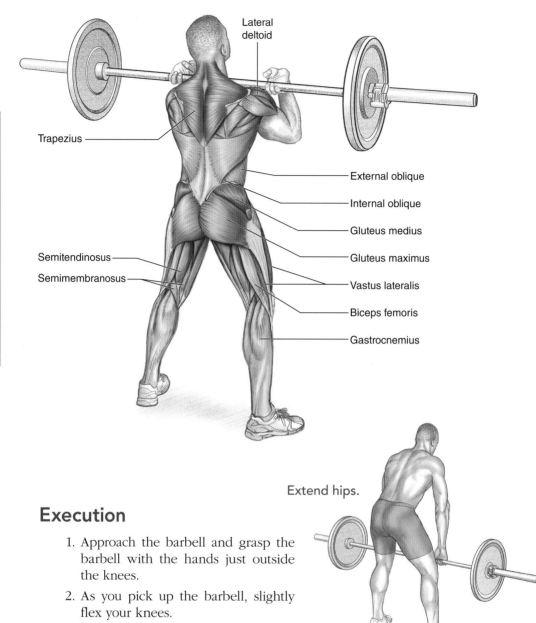

Lateral deltoid

Trapezius

External oblique

Internal oblique

Gluteus medius

Semitendinosus

Gluteus maximus

Semimembranosus

Vastus lateralis

Biceps femoris

Gastrocnemius

Extend hips.

Execution

1. Approach the barbell and grasp the barbell with the hands just outside the knees.

2. As you pick up the barbell, slightly flex your knees.

3. Moving the hips backward and maintaining the knee angle, lower the bar to a position slightly above the knees.

4. The chest should be positioned over and in front of the barbell as the upper back is straight and the lower back slightly arched. The arms should be relaxed and completely extended.

5. Extend the hips upward and forward while maintaining a slightly flexed knee angle, causing the barbell to slide up the front of the thighs.

6. Fully extend the knees and ankles as you quickly shrug the shoulders, causing the barbell to rise vertically.

7. Once the barbell reaches its highest point, rotate your elbows up and in to receive the bar. The barbell will rest along both the shoulders and clavicles.

8. Perform the prescribed number of repetitions.

Muscles Involved

Primary: Gluteus maximus, gluteus medius, semitendinosus, vastus lateralis, vastus medialis, vastus intermedius, trapezius, lateral deltoid, anterior deltoid

Secondary: Gastrocnemius, biceps femoris, semimembranosus, rectus femoris, rectus abdominis, internal oblique, external oblique

Basketball Focus

Similar to the power snatch, the power clean from hang position is an advanced exercise that requires proper technique. Use a light weight or the barbell alone when initially performing this exercise to master the technique and generate a fast barbell path. This exercise develops explosive power and total-body strength. As you become proficient in this exercise, you will develop the ability to generate greater force into the floor, which will improve your ability to jump higher and accelerate faster. The power clean is a total-body exercise that works the quadriceps, hamstrings, and abdominal muscles to stabilize the weight as it sits atop the shoulders. This is important for withstanding the physical contact that you receive when in the air, such as when attempting a layup or during a rebound.

⟨VARIATIONS⟩

Power Clean From Box

As described in the power snatch from box exercise, box height is adjusted based on the desired barbell height. The boxes can be adjusted to assume a barbell starting position above the knee, at the knee, or below the knee.

Power Clean From Floor

Starting the exercise with the barbell on the floor is the most advanced variation of the power clean. This position may be difficult for a taller athlete because it requires the greatest joint mobility and muscle flexibility for maintaining the starting position. If you can assume this starting position, your hips and shoulders need to rise together to start the first pull. As you begin to rise, the bar should stay close to the body until it is above the knees. Performing this exercise from the floor requires greater technical proficiency as well as a greater contribution of strength before the transition to the emphasis of high-speed power output.

chapter 7

PLYOMETRICS FOR A QUICKER FIRST STEP AND GAME REACTION

During competition, the player who jumps the highest and moves the quickest will have a distinct advantage over the opponent. One method of training that enhances physical abilities is plyometric exercise. Plyometric activities involve a lengthening (eccentric muscle contraction) prestretch of the muscle–tendon unit immediately followed by a rapid shortening (concentric muscle contraction) of the same muscle–tendon unit. This process occurs during the stretch–shortening cycle (SSC) and is an essential part of the plyometric training process. When plyometric exercises are performed properly, the SSC enhances the ability of the muscle–tendon unit to produce optimal force in a very brief time.

When you attempt a jump shot and miss, upon landing from this scoring attempt you might immediately jump again in an attempt to grab the rebound. When you land from the initial jump, the muscles of the lower extremities, including the quadriceps and gastrocnemius, are stretched as they lengthen (the hip and knees flex as the ankles dorsiflex) and then shorten when the immediate subsequent jump occurs during the attempt to rebound the basketball. During this process there is a brief transition from the eccentric lengthening of the muscles to the subsequent concentric shortening (contraction) of the muscles, known as the amortization phase.

The amortization phase is a quasi-isometric phase of muscle activity during which the transmission of the potential energy that occurs during the muscle lengthening is transferred as kinetic energy to be used by the contracting muscles during athletic performance. The amortization phase is critical to the success of plyometric training. The greater the time spent on the floor during the amortization phase, the greater the potential energy that will be lost as heat for exercise performance. Therefore, during plyometric activities, the rate, not the length, at which the muscle–tendon unit is stretched results in a more forceful muscle output. How quickly the stretch occurs is a factor that determines the amount of energy available for the desired explosive muscle contraction.

Plyometric exercises have been noted to bridge the gap between maximal strength levels and sport-related power and speed. You need a good base of strength and no injury before initiating plyometric training. Also be aware that optimal enhancement for athletic performance includes power training in conjunction with strength training. Power training will improve athleticism more than strength training will alone.

Following are the exercises in this chapter:

Lower-Body Plyometrics

Tuck jump
Single-leg hurdle jump
Depth jump into jump shot
Multiple-box jump
Skater hop
Split jump into run

Upper-Body Plyometrics

Pivot step to medicine ball chest pass
Medicine ball slam into vertical jump
Medicine ball push-up

TUCK JUMP

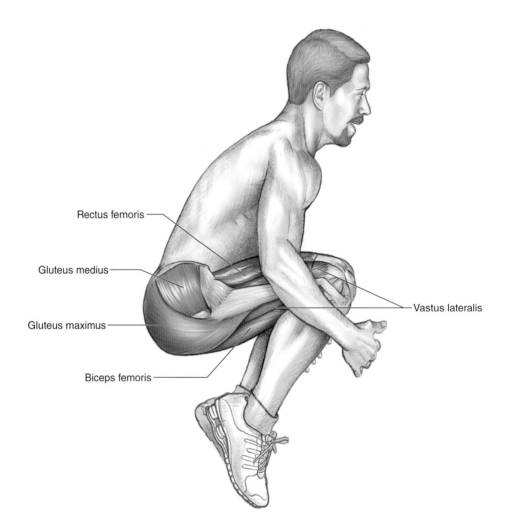

Rectus femoris

Gluteus medius

Gluteus maximus

Biceps femoris

Vastus lateralis

Execution

1. Stand erect with feet slightly wider than shoulder-width apart. Arms are at the sides of the body.

2. Flexing the knees, hips, and trunk, slowly descend toward the floor and immediately jump vertically by quickly extending the body while simultaneously throwing the arms up. Bring both knees up toward the chest (hips and knees should be at 90-degree angles) while wrapping both arms around the knees.

3. Release the arms as you extend the body. Land softly, giving way by flexing the knees, hips, and trunk to reduce impact forces. Quickly repeat and execute the jump by flexing the knees, hips, and trunk.

4. Perform for the prescribed time or number of repetitions.

Muscles Involved

Primary at takeoff: Gluteus maximus, gluteus medius, quadriceps (rectus femoris, vastus lateralis, vastus intermedius, vastus medius)

Primary at landing: Gluteus maximus, gluteus medius, quadriceps (rectus femoris, vastus lateralis, vastus intermedius, vastus medius), biceps femoris, semimembranosus, semitendinosus

Basketball Focus

The tuck jump will increase your ability to jump higher and react more quickly when going up for a rebound. Jumping is a vital component in other basketball skills, such as going for a layup, jumping to block a shot, or performing a slam dunk. Strong quadriceps, hamstrings, and gastrocnemius muscles will help you jump higher. The basic tuck jump exercise will increase your strength and ability to react quickly.

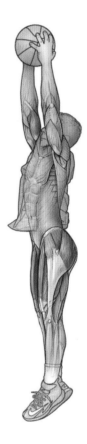

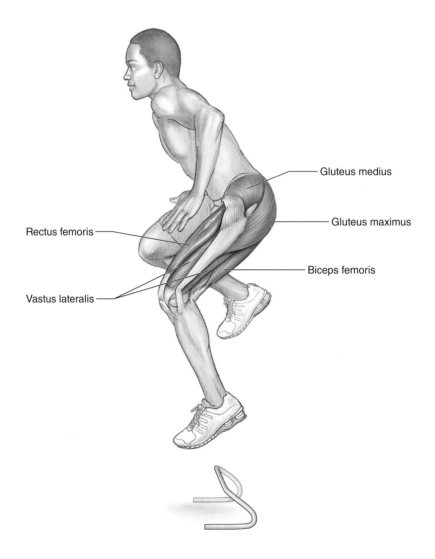

Gluteus medius

Gluteus maximus

Rectus femoris

Biceps femoris

Vastus lateralis

SAFETY TIP ▷ You must be proficient in performing double-leg hurdle jumps before attempting single-leg jumps.

Execution

1. Select an appropriate hurdle height for this exercise, such as 6- to 12-inch (15-30 cm) hurdles. Place three to five hurdles in a straight line spaced about 2 to 3 feet (60-90 cm) apart from each other.

2. Stand erect on one leg with the foot pointed straight ahead in line with the shoulders. The arms are at the sides of the body.

3. Flexing the knee of the standing leg as well as the hips and trunk, slowing descend toward the floor and immediately jump vertically off one leg. Quickly extend the body while simultaneously throwing the arms up, propelling your body over the hurdle.

4. Land softly on the floor at impact on the same leg, slightly flexing at the knee, hip, and trunk to absorb forces. After landing, immediately jump over the next hurdle with the same leg. Execute the prescribed number of hurdles or repetitions. Repeat the exercise with the opposite leg.

Muscles Involved

Primary at takeoff: Gluteus maximus, gluteus medius, quadriceps (rectus femoris, vastus lateralis, vastus intermedius, vastus medius)

Primary at landing: Gluteus maximus, gluteus medius, quadriceps (rectus femoris, vastus lateralis, vastus intermedius, vastus medius), biceps femoris, semimembranosus, semitendinosus

Basketball Focus

Single-leg hurdle jumps improve your ability to quickly jump off the floor. This will help you more quickly push off during a layup or jump up for a rebound. Explosiveness when jumping off one leg is necessary in basketball. If hurdles are not available, you can perform this exercise without them by jumping as high as you can forward.

◄ VARIATION ►

Double-Leg Hurdle Jump

Perform the same exercise but use both legs to propel your body over the hurdle.

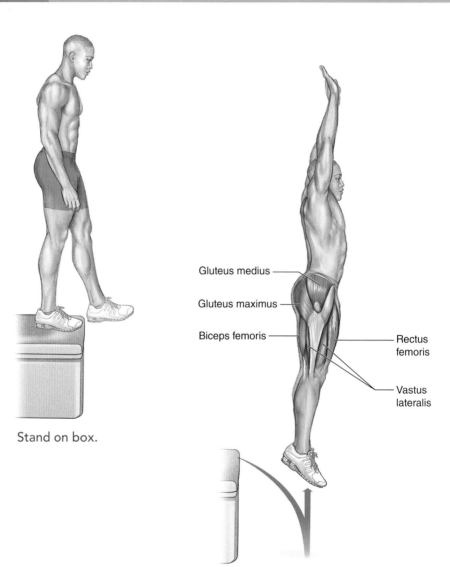

Stand on box.

Gluteus medius
Gluteus maximus
Biceps femoris
Rectus femoris
Vastus lateralis

Execution

1. Stand erect on top of a box of a prescribed height (12-30 in., or 30-75 cm), depending on strength and athletic ability. Position your body close to the edge of the box and step (do not jump) forward to lower your body toward the floor.

2. Make contact with the floor simultaneously with both feet and immediately jump quickly to simulate a jump shot.

3. Perform for the prescribed time or number of repetitions.

Muscles Involved

Primary at takeoff: Gluteus maximus, gluteus medius, quadriceps (rectus femoris, vastus lateralis, vastus intermedius, vastus medius)

Primary at landing: Gluteus maximus, gluteus medius, quadriceps (rectus femoris, vastus lateralis, vastus intermedius, vastus medius), biceps femoris, semimembranosus, semitendinosus

Basketball Focus

A depth jump into a jump shot will improve your ability to shoot over an opponent while simulating a jump shot. Choose a box of an appropriate height until you develop significant strength and athletic ability. Jumping from a height will help you decelerate by lengthening the quadriceps and gastrocnemius and applying force into the floor to jump as high as possible. Simulating the jump shot improves the ability to mimic game-specific actions.

◀ VARIATION ▶

Low-Box Depth Jump Into Jump Shot

Perform the same exercise off a smaller box until you build significant strength and athletic ability.

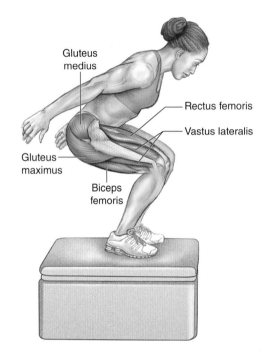

Gluteus
medius

Rectus femoris

Vastus lateralis

Gluteus
maximus

Biceps
femoris

Execution

1. Stand erect facing a row of boxes (usually two to four) of a prescribed height (12-30 in., or 30-75 cm) depending on strength and athletic ability. Position your body 1 to 2 feet (30-60 cm) from the first box with your feet approximately shoulder-width apart.

2. Flexing the knees, hips, and trunk, slowly descend toward the floor and immediately jump on the first box by quickly extending your body while simultaneously throwing the arms upward. Land softly on the box, giving way by flexing the knees, hips, and trunk to reduce impact forces.

3. Once you land on the first box, immediately jump off the box toward the floor. As you make contact, quickly jump onto next box and continue this process for the prescribed number of boxes.

Muscles Involved

Primary at takeoff: Gluteus maximus, gluteus medius, quadriceps (rectus femoris, vastus lateralis, vastus intermedius, vastus medius)

Primary at landing: Gluteus maximus, gluteus medius, quadriceps (rectus femoris, vastus lateralis, vastus intermedius, vastus medius), biceps femoris, semimembranosus, semitendinosus

Basketball Focus

Multiple-box jumps help you develop quicker reaction off the floor so that you can jump higher for rebounds and jump shots and improve quickness on the court. Explosiveness off the floor allows you to beat your opponent to the basket or when running to get a loose ball. The quicker reaction off the floor will also help when changing direction to avoid a defender or looking to drop step to pass the ball.

⟨ VARIATION ⟩

Long Jump

Simulate the box jump exercise but go for distance. Perform three or four long jumps, focusing on quickly jumping off the floor.

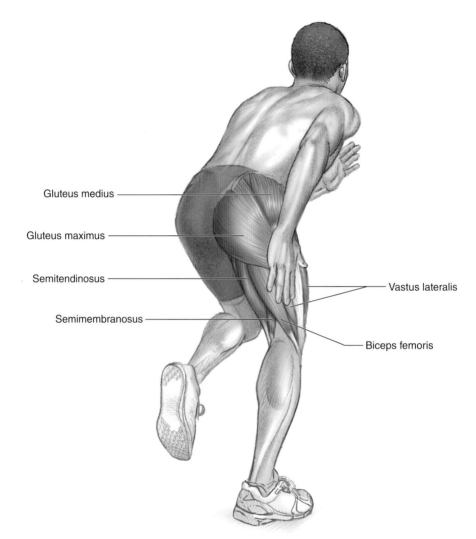

Gluteus medius

Gluteus maximus

Semitendinosus

Semimembranosus

Vastus lateralis

Biceps femoris

Execution

1. Face forward and stand erect on the right leg with the left leg behind and the tip of the left foot touching the floor.

2. Flexing the knee and hip of the right leg, jump to the left and land softly on the left leg by flexing the knee and hip.

3. Immediately after landing, bring the right leg behind the left leg with the tip of the right foot touching the floor and immediately jump to the right, landing on the right leg. The upper body faces forward throughout the exercise.

4. Begin the exercise with small lateral jumps and then increase the distance of the lateral jumps.

5. Perform the prescribed number of repetitions.

Muscles Involved

Primary at takeoff: Gluteus maximus, gluteus medius, quadriceps (rectus femoris, vastus lateralis, vastus intermedius, vastus medius), tensor fasciae latae

Primary at landing: Gluteus maximus, gluteus medius, quadriceps (rectus femoris, vastus lateralis, vastus intermedius, vastus medius), tensor fasciae latae, biceps femoris, semimembranosus, semitendinosus

Basketball Focus

This exercise improves your ability to make quicker cuts on the court and to become more explosive laterally. You must make quick cuts to get around a defender and be able to react quickly when changing directions. Strong lateral hip muscles—the gluteus medius, gluteus maximus, vastus lateralis, and tensor fasciae latae—will help you generate more force into the floor to avoid a defender when making quick changes of direction or performing a jab step. Strong lateral hip muscles will also help prevent knee injuries by absorbing some of the force when you make these quick cutting motions or handle a rebound.

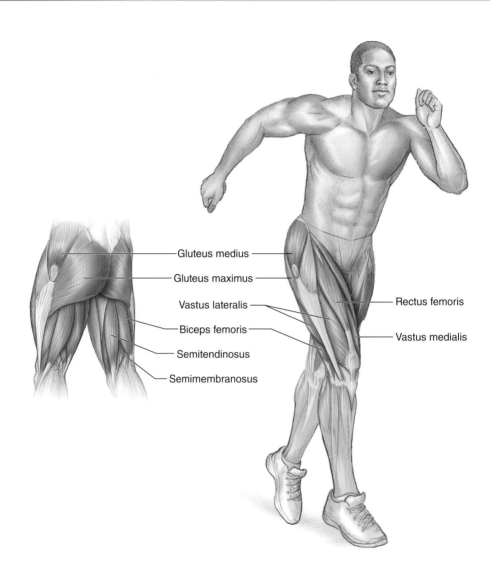

Gluteus medius

Gluteus maximus

Vastus lateralis

Biceps femoris

Semitendinosus

Semimembranosus

Rectus femoris

Vastus medialis

Execution

1. Assume a split squat stance with the front leg extended with both the hip and knee flexed at 90 degrees and the front foot pointed straight ahead. The rear leg should be positioned with the knee flexed at 90 degrees pointing toward the floor in line with the hips and shoulders (half-kneeling position).

2. Bounce up and down twice without leaving the floor, then immediately jump as vertically and as high as possible while maintaining the split squat position. The arms should be below shoulder height and the hands placed on the hips to emphasize the use of the legs.

3. On the landing, maintain the split squat position, bending the knees to absorb the forces, and immediately sprint the prescribed distance.

4. Continue the exercise, alternating right and left legs in the forward position for the prescribed number of repetitions and distance.

Muscles Involved

Primary at takeoff: Gluteus maximus, gluteus medius, quadriceps (rectus femoris, vastus lateralis, vastus intermedius, vastus medius)

Primary at landing: Gluteus maximus, gluteus medius, quadriceps (rectus femoris, vastus lateralis, vastus intermedius, vastus medius), biceps femoris, semimembranosus, semitendinosus

Basketball Focus

This exercise will help you develop a quicker first step and be more explosive when running on the court. In any sport, having a quick first step is vital to beating an opponent. This exercise simulates coming down with a rebound and taking off on a fast break. It also teaches you to use both legs to generate force into the floor and then react to a forward sprinting movement. Going from a split position to a run forces you to use balance and momentum to accelerate. To avoid injury, you need to achieve proper technique when doing the split jump.

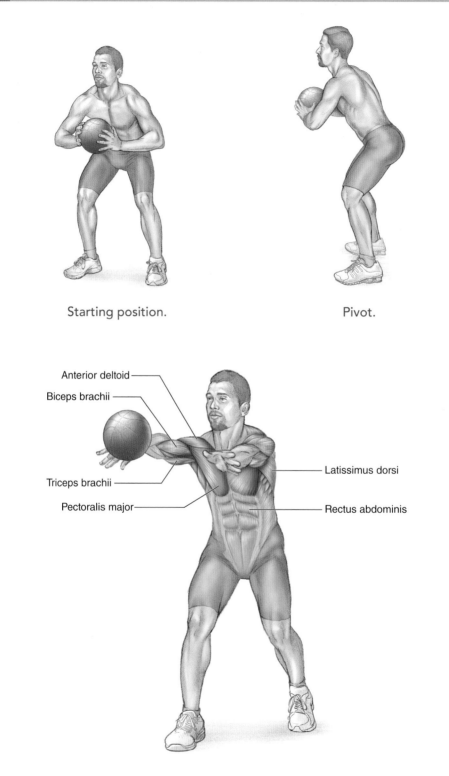

Starting position.

Pivot.

Anterior deltoid

Biceps brachii

Triceps brachii

Pectoralis major

Latissimus dorsi

Rectus abdominis

Execution

1. Facing either a wall or a partner, stand erect with both feet approximately shoulder-width apart. Hold a medicine ball of a prescribed weight. Slightly bend the hips and knees in preparation for the exercise.

2. Hold the medicine ball close to your chest with the elbows bent. Pivot on the right foot to the right then immediately return to the starting position by pivoting (rotating) to the left and forward.

3. Forcefully extend both arms as you throw the medicine ball into the wall or to your partner.

4. As the medicine ball returns to you, slowly decelerate the ball back to your chest.

5. Perform to both the right and the left the prescribed number of repetitions or throws.

Muscles Involved

Primary: Pectoralis major, pectoralis minor, triceps brachii, anterior deltoid

Secondary: Biceps brachii, latissimus dorsi, rectus abdominis

Basketball Focus

This exercise develops a quick jab step and an explosive chest pass. Generating upper-body force to pass a basketball more quickly gives you the edge to set up the shot by avoiding the defender trying to intercept the pass. Working on footwork to change direction and juke an opponent will allow easier transition to the basket.

Slam.

Triceps brachii

Pectoralis major

Latissimus dorsi

Rectus abdominis

Gluteus medius

Tensor fasciae latae

Gluteus maximus

Rectus femoris

Biceps femoris

Vastus lateralis

Execution

1. Stand erect with feet shoulder-width apart. Hold a medicine ball of a prescribed weight in both hands, arms fully extended overhead.

2. Rise onto the balls of the feet and hold for two seconds. Forcibly throw the medicine ball to the floor, simultaneously bending your knees as you release the ball.

3. At the time the thrown medicine ball makes floor contact, immediately jump as high as you can.

4. Land softly in a proper defensive stance position.

5. Perform the prescribed number of repetitions or throws.

Muscles Involved

Primary at takeoff: Gluteus maximus, gluteus medius, quadriceps (rectus femoris, vastus lateralis, vastus intermedius, vastus medius), tensor fasciae latae

Primary at landing: Gluteus maximus, gluteus medius, quadriceps (rectus femoris, vastus lateralis, vastus intermedius, vastus medius), tensor fasciae latae, biceps femoris, semimembranosus, semitendinosus

Secondary: Biceps brachii, latissimus dorsi, rectus abdominis, pectoralis major, triceps brachii, anterior deltoid

Basketball Focus

This exercise develops total-body power so that you jump higher and improve core strength, leading to more power when driving to the hoop. This is seen when reaching up for a missed shot and then coming down with it and jumping up again for a slam dunk. Quickly reacting off the floor from a jump will give you an edge in jumping higher than your opponent.

Lower chest to ball.

Latissimus dorsi

Anterior deltoid

Biceps brachii

Pectoralis major

Rectus abdominis

Triceps brachii

Execution

1. Assume a push-up position with a medicine ball placed on the floor between your arms and below your chest.

2. Initiate a push-up by lowering the chest toward the medicine ball until the chest slightly touches the medicine ball.

3. Once the chest touches the medicine ball, push away from the floor with enough force for the hands to leave the floor and immediately place them on the top of the medicine ball.

4. As the body lowers and the chest again touches the medicine ball, forcibly push the hands off the medicine ball and stabilize the body after landing on the floor in the starting push-up position.

5. Perform the prescribed number of repetitions.

Muscles Involved

Primary: Pectoralis major, pectoralis minor, triceps brachii, anterior deltoid

Secondary: Biceps brachii, latissimus dorsi, rectus abdominis

Basketball Focus

Explosive upper-body strength helps you pass the ball much more quickly. A strong upper body also helps you grab for rebounds or go for a loose ball. Defending and boxing out an opponent both require you to stabilize your position and not be bumped out of position. When two players have both their hands on the ball after a rebound, the athlete with the stronger upper body tends to win the battle.

chapter 8

REHABILITATION FOR OPTIMAL RETURN TO PLAY

ecause all injuries vary in severity and there is a possibility of associated anatomical injury or preexisting pathology, you should seek the opinion of a qualified medical practitioner before initiating a rehabilitation program or continuing performance-enhancing training. This chapter discusses venues of care for pathologies at the ankle, knee, and shoulder.

ANKLE SPRAINS

Ligamentous ankle sprains occur in the general public at a rate of 30,000 per day and are ranked as the most common basketball-related injuries to the foot and ankle. The majority of sprains involve the anterior talofibular ligament (ATFL), calcaneal fibular ligament (CFL), and posterior talofibular ligament (PTFL) (figure 8.1). A typical mechanism of injury occurs with a combined motion of ankle plantar flexion and inversion, a foot position that would occur when landing on an opponent's foot. This vulnerable position of the foot and ankle can happen while running and jumping and during cutting activities. Once an ankle sprain does occur, a qualified physician should evaluate the injury and recommend treatment.

The severity of an ankle sprain is classified by the physiological pathology, physical exam, and functional limitation. Traditionally, there are three classifications of ankle sprains, and rehabilitation depends on the severity of the sprain (table 8.1).

A grade 1 (mild) ankle sprain occurs when there is a mild stretch to ligamentous structures without functional ankle instability with only single-ligament involvement. A physical exam will reveal no or minimal swelling or ecchymosis (bruising) and tenderness to palpation about the involved ligament. Clinical special tests will be negative. You will have no or minimal functional limitations but may have mild gait deviations. Aggressive rehabilitation of approximately one week will help heal the injury.

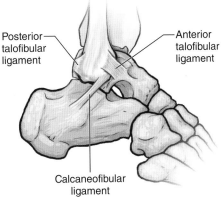

Figure 8.1   Ligaments of the ankle.

Table 8.1 Ankle Sprains

	Pathology	Physical exam	Functional limitations	Rehabilitation
Grade 1 (mild) ankle sprain	Mild stretch to ligaments No functional ankle instability Single-ligament involvement	No or minimal swelling or ecchymosis Tenderness around the ligament Negative clinical special tests	No or minimal limitations Mild gait deviations	Aggressive (approximately 1 week)
Grade 2 (moderate) ankle sprain	Partial tearing of ligaments Mild to moderate ankle instability Single- or multiple-ligament involvement	Ankle swelling and ecchymosis Tenderness around the ligament Positive clinical special tests for ligamentous laxity	Occasional ROM deficits Strength deficits Inability to raise heel unilaterally Gait deviations Inability to jump or run	Conservative (approximately 3 to 4 weeks)
Grade 3 (severe) ankle sprain	Complete tear of ligament Gross ankle instability Single- or multiple-ligament involvement	Moderate swelling and ecchymosis Tenderness around ligament and malleoli Positive clinical special tests for ligamentous laxity Guarding and pain	ROM and ankle strength deficits Gait deviations Inability to bear weight Requires assistive device	Very conservative (approximately 5 to 12 weeks)

A grade 2 (moderate) ankle sprain occurs when there is partial tearing of the involved ligaments with mild to moderate ankle instability. One or more ligaments may be involved. A physical exam will show ankle swelling and ecchymosis and tenderness to palpation about the involved ligament. Clinical special tests will be positive for ligamentous laxity. You will have occasional range of motion (ROM) deficits and strength deficits; you might be unable to raise the heel unilaterally. You will have gait deviations and an inability to jump or run. Conservative rehabilitation of approximately three to four weeks will help heal the injury.

A grade 3 (severe) ankle sprain occurs when there is a complete tear of the ligament with gross ankle instability. One or more ligaments may be involved. A physical exam will show moderate swelling and ecchymosis and tenderness to palpation about the involved ligament or malleoli. Clinical special tests will be positive for ligamentous laxity (guarding and pain present). You will have deficits in ROM and ankle strength and gait deviations, including an inability to bear weight; an assistive device will be required. Very conservative rehabilitation (approximately 5 to 12 weeks) will help heal the injury.

Rehabilitation goals of an acute ankle sprain should focus on reducing the inflammatory process, reducing pain, promoting repair, and remodeling collagen fibers. The acronym PRICE is readily used during the acute treatment and management of ankle sprains.

Protect: Use ankle bracing or assistive devices to alleviate stress and pain.

Rest: Prevent undue tissue damage.

Ice: Decrease pain and blood flow, reducing bruising.

Compression: Increase external pressure to decrease swelling.

Elevation: Decrease swelling and assist venous and lymphatic return.

The introduction of exercise and functional activities depends on the stage of healing. Controlled stresses via exercise and weight-bearing activities will promote healing; however, excessive loading can interfere with healing and prolong the inflammatory process. As pain and swelling subside, you may perform more aggressive strengthening and weight-bearing tasks.

The primary focus should be on restoring ankle ROM. Ankle dorsiflexion (DF) and plantar flexion (PF) can be treated aggressively; however, ankle inversion (IV) and eversion (EV) should be treated as tolerated. Ankle ROM can be restored via stretching (gastrocnemius and soleus muscle complex) and via soft tissue massage to the surrounding muscle groups (gastrocnemius, soleus, peroneals, tibialis posterior, flexor digitorum longus, and flexor hallucis longus).

After ROM is normalized, ankle strengthening should be progressed. Open-chain exercises will advance to closed-chain exercises as weight bearing is tolerated well.

Restoration of balance and proprioception are imperative for preventing future ankle sprains and are the foundation for advanced performance. When balance and proprioception are mastered, advanced rehabilitation and conditioning may be integrated into the treatment program. A dynamic warm-up, agility, jogging, sagittal-plane running, jumping, cutting and change of direction, and deceleration training will now be incorporated into the treatment progression.

Recurrent ankle sprains are usually related to insufficient balance or proprioception, strength, and poor quality of movement or execution of a task. Recurrent ankle sprains occurring from these deficits may require long-term use of external supports such as athletic taping or bracing. Progressive balance or proprioception and strength training are required in players with chronic ankle dysfunction.

The balance, proprioceptive, and strengthening exercises in this chapter include the following:

Ankle Balance

Single-leg stance
Rocker board

Ankle Proprioception

Seated Physioball perturbation
Hopping
Contralateral kick

Ankle Strengthening

Resistive ankle motion
Standing heel raise
Band lateral walk

Execution

1. Stand erect with full body weight distributed through affected lower extremity.

2. Keeping a slight bend in the knee, shift all the body weight onto the affected lower extremity. During balance activity, try to maintain a fixed posture.

3. To advance this exercise, introduce an unstable surface such as a foam pad, Dynadisc, or BOSU or close your eyes.

Muscles Involved

Primary: Gastrocnemius, soleus, tibialis anterior, extensor hallucis longus, extensor digitorum longus, flexor hallucis longus, flexor digitorum longus, tibialis posterior, peroneals, interossei, lumbricals

Secondary: Gluteus maximus, gluteus medius, hamstrings (semitendinosus, semimembranosus, biceps femoris), quadriceps (rectus femoris, vastus lateralis, vastus medialis, vastus intermedius), erector spinae (iliocostalis, longissimus, spinalis), rectus abdominis

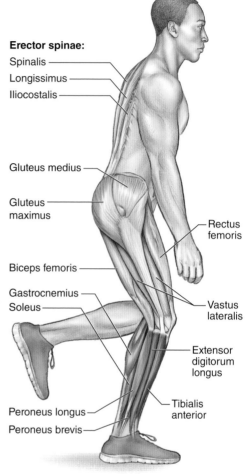

Erector spinae:
Spinalis
Longissimus
Iliocostalis

Gluteus medius

Gluteus maximus

Rectus femoris

Biceps femoris

Gastrocnemius
Soleus

Vastus lateralis

Extensor digitorum longus

Peroneus longus
Peroneus brevis

Tibialis anterior

Basketball Focus

Single-leg balance is a key skill required in basketball players. It is important during the running cycle when one leg is in contact with the floor and during unilateral jumping and landing (layup). When you cut to avoid an opponent, ankle stability is important for maintaining positioning and reacting to any unforeseen obstacles. Many players injure their ankles when coming down from a rebound when they land on an opponent's foot. Your ability to maintain stability on an unstable surface will help you react and avoid injury.

Execution

1. Stand erect on a rocker board or BOSU with full body weight distributed evenly through both legs. The unstable surface will challenge medial and lateral or anterior and posterior stability.

2. Keeping a slight bend in the knees, slowly lower into a minisquat position. During the balance activity, try to maintain fixed posture and keep the board in a neutral position.

3. To advance this exercise, introduce external forces such as perturbations or catching a chest pass.

Muscles Involved

Primary: Gastrocnemius, soleus, tibialis anterior, extensor hallucis longus, extensor digitorum longus, flexor hallucis longus, flexor digitorum longus, tibialis posterior, peroneals, interossei, lumbricals

Secondary: Gluteus maximus, gluteus medius, hamstrings (semitendinosus, semimembranosus, biceps femoris), quadriceps (rectus femoris, vastus lateralis, vastus medialis, vastus intermedius), erector spinae (iliocostalis, longissimus, spinalis), rectus abdominis

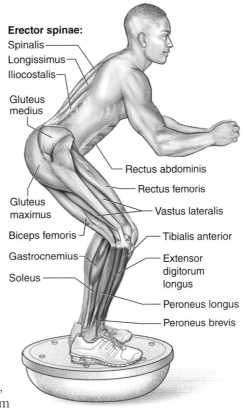

Erector spinae:
Spinalis
Longissimus
Iliocostalis

Gluteus medius

Gluteus maximus

Biceps femoris

Gastrocnemius

Soleus

Rectus abdominis

Rectus femoris

Vastus lateralis

Tibialis anterior

Extensor digitorum longus

Peroneus longus

Peroneus brevis

Basketball Focus

Maintaining balance while in a minisquat is functional. It simulates starting position for free throw and the return position from a jump. Your ability to maintain balance and strength in both ankles and quads will help you be more explosive when you have to change direction or drive to the basket. As a preventive measure, maintain your strength and stability in the ankles throughout the season.

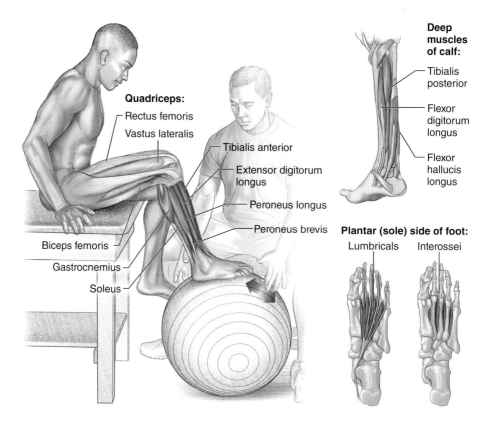

Quadriceps:
Rectus femoris
Vastus lateralis

Tibialis anterior
Extensor digitorum longus
Peroneus longus
Peroneus brevis

Biceps femoris
Gastrocnemius
Soleus

Deep muscles of calf:
Tibialis posterior
Flexor digitorum longus
Flexor hallucis longus

Plantar (sole) side of foot:
Lumbricals   Interossei

Execution

1. This exercise is used during the acute phase of ankle rehabilitation. Sit on the edge of a table with your foot resting on a Physioball in a neutral position.

2. Maintain the neutral position of the foot and ankle as a clinician provides perturbations to the Physioball.

3. To advance the exercise, the clinician moves from predicted patterns to unpredicted patterns of perturbation or you close your eyes.

Muscles Involved

Primary: Gastrocnemius, soleus, tibialis anterior, extensor hallucis longus, extensor digitorum longus, flexor hallucis longus, flexor digitorum longus, tibialis posterior, peroneals, interossei, lumbricals

Secondary: Hamstrings (semitendinosus, semimembranosus, biceps femoris), quadriceps (rectus femoris, vastus lateralis, vastus medialis, vastus intermedius)

Basketball Focus

Proprioception is important in ankle dysfunction. During every step of basketball, you need to have a sense of body awareness during running, jumping, cutting, and deceleration tasks. Because of the fast pace of basketball and the changes in direction throughout the game, your ankles and overall conditioning are important for keeping you on the court and not on the bench with injuries. The quick movements in basketball—the jab step or a move off a pick-and-roll, for example—require your ankles to withstand the forces placed on them.

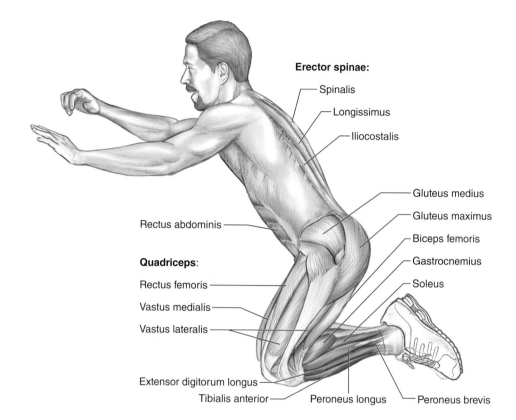

Erector spinae:
- Spinalis
- Longissimus
- Iliocostalis

Gluteus medius

Gluteus maximus

Rectus abdominis

Biceps femoris

Gastrocnemius

Quadriceps:

Soleus

Rectus femoris

Vastus medialis

Vastus lateralis

Extensor digitorum longus

Tibialis anterior

Peroneus longus

Peroneus brevis

Execution

1. Assume a standing position with a slight bend in the knees.

2. Maintaining the slight bend in the knees, sling the arms back and hop forward. Land with the knees bent and the hips back. Jump as far as possible while maintaining a good landing position.

3. To advance the exercise, hop off two legs and land on two legs, then hop off two legs and land on one leg, then hop off one leg and land on one leg. You can advance the exercise by hopping forward and backward and side to side using hurdles or boxes.

Muscles Involved

Primary: Gastrocnemius, soleus, tibialis anterior, extensor hallucis longus, extensor digitorum longus, flexor hallucis longus, flexor digitorum longus, tibialis posterior, peroneals, interossei, lumbricals

Secondary: Hamstrings (semitendinosus, semimembranosus, biceps femoris), quadriceps (rectus femoris, vastus lateralis, vastus medialis, vastus intermedius), gluteus maximus, gluteus medius, rectus abdominis, erector spinae (iliocostalis, longissimus, spinalis)

Basketball Focus

Hopping promotes frontal and sagittal propulsion, deceleration ability, and balance and proprioception in the lower extremities. Reacting quickly off the floor will help you jump and run more quickly. The ability to quickly react off the floor can make the difference between getting a rebound and being beat to the ball.

Execution

1. Balance on the affected lower extremity with the foot of the noninjured leg attached to a resistance band at floor level. The band should be around the ankle of the noninjured leg.

2. Maintaining balance of the affected lower extremity, kick with the noninjured leg against the resistance band in the sagittal and horizontal planes of motion (forward, backward, and side to side).

3. To advance the exercise, increase the resistance of the band or the speed of the kicks.

Muscles Involved

Primary: Gastrocnemius, soleus, tibialis anterior, extensor hallucis longus, extensor digitorum longus, flexor hallucis longus, flexor digitorum longus, tibialis posterior, peroneals, interossei, lumbricals

Secondary: Gluteus maximus, gluteus medius, hamstrings (semitendinosus, semimembranosus, biceps femoris), quadriceps (rectus femoris, vastus lateralis, vastus medialis, vastus intermedius), rectus abdominis

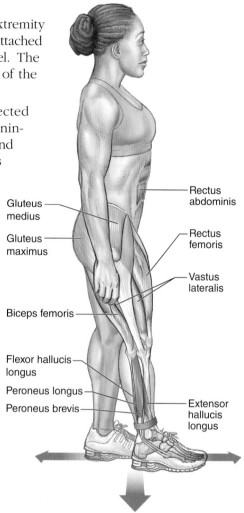

Gluteus medius
Gluteus maximus
Biceps femoris
Flexor hallucis longus
Peroneus longus
Peroneus brevis
Rectus abdominis
Rectus femoris
Vastus lateralis
Extensor hallucis longus

Basketball Focus

Unilateral proprioception is important for maintaining body awareness during unilateral standing tasks such as running. When you drive to the basket for a layup or shoot off balance, your ability to stabilize and push off the lower leg is vital to the success of the shot. Landing from a rebound or running after a loose ball requires you to control the landing or be explosive to get to the ball.

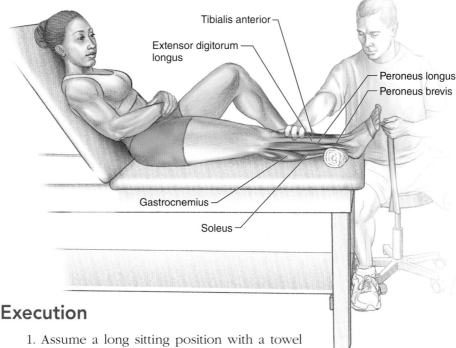

Tibialis anterior

Extensor digitorum longus

Peroneus longus
Peroneus brevis

Gastrocnemius

Soleus

Execution

1. Assume a long sitting position with a towel roll placed under the ankle, which is in neutral position.
2. Attach a resistance band around the foot. Hold the other end of the band in your hands.
3. Moving against the resistance of the band, complete the ankle range of motion (dorsiflexion, plantar flexion, inversion, and eversion).
4. To advance the exercise, increase the resistance of the band.

Muscles Involved

Primary: Gastrocnemius, soleus, tibialis anterior, tibialis posterior, peroneals

Secondary: Extensor hallucis longus, extensor digitorum longus, flexor hallucis longus, flexor digitorum longus, interossei, lumbricals

Basketball Focus

Ankle strength is the primary focus for stability of the ankle during running, jumping, and cutting or changing direction. The most common injury in basketball is an ankle sprain. Ankle sprains usually occur when players fight for a rebound and one player lands on the opponent's foot. Ankle strength is often overlooked when it comes to exercise and training for basketball. If you don't want to miss playing time due to an ankle sprain, you need to spend the recommended time strengthening the muscles surrounding the ankles.

Execution

1. Stand with the knees fully extended. If desired, hold a dumbbell in each hand.
2. Lift the heels off the floor and slowly return to the starting position.
3. To advance the exercise, add more weight to the shoulders.

Muscles Involved

Primary: Gastrocnemius, soleus, peroneals

Secondary: Tibialis anterior, tibialis posterior, extensor hallucis longus, extensor digitorum longus, flexor hallucis longus, flexor digitorum longus, interossei, lumbricals

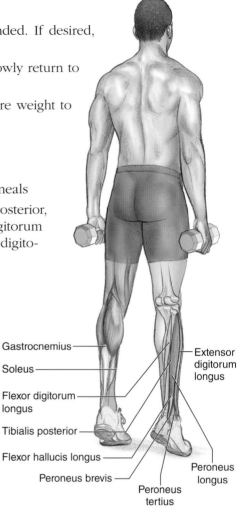

Gastrocnemius

Soleus

Flexor digitorum longus

Tibialis posterior

Flexor hallucis longus

Peroneus brevis

Peroneus tertius

Extensor digitorum longus

Peroneus longus

Basketball Focus

Plantar flexion strength is vital in producing the force output to execute plyometric activities such as shooting and jumping. The gastrocnemius muscles of the calves give you the ability to push off the floor to run faster and jump higher. To become explosive in these movements, you need to develop the elastic ability in the muscle as well as the strength.

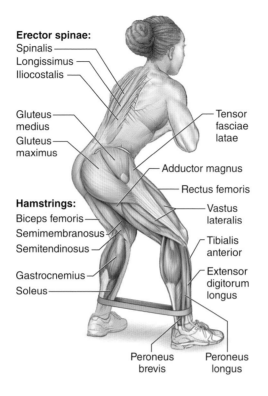

Erector spinae:
Spinalis
Longissimus
Iliocostalis

Gluteus medius
Gluteus maximus

Hamstrings:
Biceps femoris
Semimembranosus
Semitendinosus

Gastrocnemius
Soleus

Tensor fasciae latae

Adductor magnus
Rectus femoris
Vastus lateralis

Tibialis anterior

Extensor digitorum longus

Peroneus brevis
Peroneus longus

Execution

1. Stand with your knees slightly bent in a minisquat position. Place a resistance band around the ankles.
2. Maintaining the squat position and neutral position of the feet, walk sideways against the pull of the resistance band.

Muscles Involved

Primary: Gastrocnemius, soleus, peroneals, tibialis anterior, tibialis posterior, extensor hallucis longus, extensor digitorum longus, flexor hallucis longus, flexor digitorum longus, interossei, lumbricals

Secondary: Hip adductors, hamstrings (semitendinosus, semimembranosus, biceps femoris), quadriceps (rectus femoris, vastus lateralis, vastus medialis, vastus intermedius), gluteus maximus, gluteus medius, rectus abdominis, erector spinae (iliocostalis, longissimus, spinalis)

Basketball Focus

The lateral band walk develops lower-extremity strength and lateral ankle stabilization to reinforce strength and proprioception for optimal play and injury prevention during all facets of basketball. Lateral hip strength allows more stability and explosiveness at the hips when cutting to avoid an opponent. The strength developed through this exercise also helps you maintain a solid athletic position to drive to the hoop or go against a defender.

JUMPER'S KNEE

Jumper's knee is an injury or inflammatory condition that presents as anterior knee pain often with a stiff and aching quality. Palpation will reveal the location of the pain at the site of the patella. Often this pain is pronounced at the inferior aspect of the tendon at the site of its insertion into the tibial tubercle. Jumper's knee may consist of a patellar tendinopathy, patellar tendinosis, or patellar tendinitis due to the repetitive stress placed on the extensor mechanism of the knee that occurs during jumping activities. This is a condition that refers to the stress overload associated with repetitive jumping. Rarely is a specific incident of injury described.

The mechanical loads that are applied to the patella appear to be greater on landing from a jump than on the takeoff because of the eccentric muscle contraction that occurs at the quadriceps during landing rather than the concentric muscle contraction that occurs during jumping. These stressful eccentric muscle contractions may exert the high-tension repeated loads that lead to injury. The physical characteristics linked to jumper's knee may include poor general physical condition (overweight), quadriceps and hamstring weakness, weakness in the gluteal muscle, and poor mobility and flexibility in the hip flexor, quadriceps, hamstring, and ankle.

Rehabilitation goals should focus on reducing the inflammatory process; reducing pain; promoting repair and remodeling of collagen fibers; and restoring range of motion, strength, stability, and flexibility for an eventual safe return to play. Considerations in the care of this knee condition should include the following:

- Protect the knee and use a patella strap or device to alleviate stress and pain.
- Rest when appropriate to prevent further undue tissue damage.
- Use ice to decrease pain and blood flow, reducing bruising.
- Restore knee range of motion both passively and actively.
- Restore strength, including the extensor muscles, hamstrings, and muscles of the hips, ankles, and core.
- Restore joint mobility and flexibility, including the hips (emphasize the hip flexors and hamstrings), knees, and ankles.
- Restore joint proprioception, including the entire lower extremity.

Following are the exercises in this section:

Mat walk
Single-leg stance on unstable surface
Eccentric leg press
Body-weight squat
Step-down
Box jump

Execution

1. Stand erect on the lateral edge of a thin mat with a length of approximately 5 to 10 yards or meters.

2. Walk with one foot placed in front of the other in tightrope fashion. One half of the foot, divided by the midline, is on the mat; the other half is off the mat. Walk the length of the mat. Do not allow either foot to touch the floor as you walk the length of the mat.

3. Perform the prescribed number of mat walks.

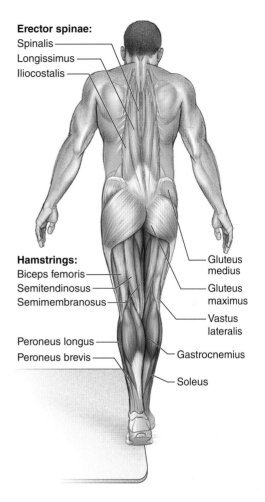

Erector spinae:
Spinalis
Longissimus
Iliocostalis

Hamstrings:
Biceps femoris
Semitendinosus
Semimembranosus

Peroneus longus
Peroneus brevis

Gluteus medius
Gluteus maximus
Vastus lateralis
Gastrocnemius
Soleus

Muscles Involved

Primary: Gastrocnemius, soleus, tibialis anterior, extensor hallucis longus, extensor digitorum longus, flexor hallucis longus, flexor digitorum longus, tibialis posterior, peroneals, interossei, lumbricals

Secondary: Gluteus maximus, gluteus medius, hamstrings (semitendinosus, semimembranosus, biceps femoris), quadriceps (rectus femoris, vastus lateralis, vastus medialis, vastus intermedius), erector spinae (iliocostalis, longissimus, spinalis), rectus abdominis

Basketball Focus

Maintaining balance during movement is essential for changing direction or for recovering in specific situations such as cutting quickly to avoid a defender when driving to the basket to throw your center of mass outside your base of support.

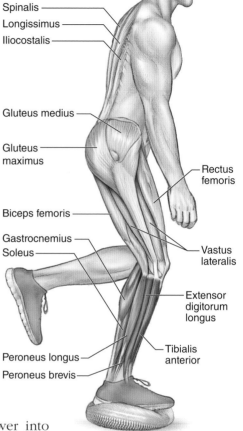

Erector spinae:
Spinalis
Longissimus
Iliocostalis

Gluteus medius

Gluteus maximus

Rectus femoris

Biceps femoris

Gastrocnemius
Soleus

Vastus lateralis

Extensor digitorum longus

Peroneus longus
Peroneus brevis

Tibialis anterior

Execution

1. Stand erect on an unstable surface such as a BOSU, Dynadisc, or foam pad with all body weight distributed through the affected lower extremity. The other leg is lifted.

2. Slightly bend the knee and lower into a minisquat. Balance and maintain a fixed posture.

3. If the bent-knee position is painful, start the exercise with a straight leg and progress to a pain-free slightly bent knee.

4. Perform the prescribed number of timed bouts.

Muscles Involved

Primary: Gastrocnemius, soleus, tibialis anterior, extensor hallucis longus, extensor digitorum longus, flexor hallucis longus, flexor digitorum longus, tibialis posterior, peroneals, interossei, lumbricals

Secondary: Gluteus maximus, gluteus medius, hamstrings (semitendinosus, semimembranosus, biceps femoris), quadriceps (rectus femoris, vastus lateralis, vastus medialis, vastus intermedius), erector spinae (iliocostalis, longissimus, spinalis), rectus abdominis

Basketball Focus

Balance while in a minisquat is functional. It simulates the starting position for the free throw and the return position from a jump. The ability to stand on one leg strengthens the quadriceps and aids in developing stability in the knee and ankle. You will benefit from developing generating power to jump off a single leg when you drive to the basket for a layup or when you are being defended on the boards.

⟨VARIATIONS⟩

Single-Leg Stance

To simplify the exercise, perform the single-leg stance on the floor.

Single-Leg Stance With Tap

Have a coach or training partner tap you from side to side, forcing you to further control your body and not lose your balance.

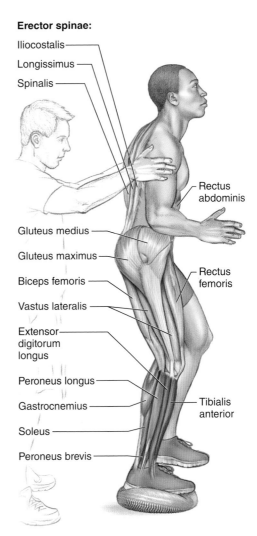

Erector spinae:

Iliocostalis

Longissimus

Spinalis

Rectus abdominis

Gluteus medius

Gluteus maximus

Rectus femoris

Biceps femoris

Vastus lateralis

Extensor digitorum longus

Peroneus longus

Gastrocnemius

Tibialis anterior

Soleus

Peroneus brevis

Hamstrings:
Biceps femoris   Semimembranosus
Semitendinosus
Gastrocnemius

Quadriceps:
Vastus lateralis
Rectus femoris
Vastus medialis

Gluteus maximus   Gluteus medius

Execution

1. Lie or sit in the leg press machine depending on the type of machine. Place your feet approximately shoulder-width apart with the toes turned out slightly. Select a weight less than your body weight.
2. Push both legs until they are fully extended.
3. Over a count of eight, slowly lower the weight using only the injured leg to starting position.
4. Perform the prescribed number of repetitions and switch legs.

Muscles Involved

Primary: Quadriceps (rectus femoris, vastus lateralis, vastus medialis, vastus intermedius), hamstrings (semitendinosus, semimembranosus, biceps femoris), gluteus maximus

Secondary: Gastrocnemius, gluteus medius, gluteus minimus

Basketball Focus

Not only does eccentric strength enhancement help resolve jumper's knee, but it also provides enhanced strength and stability during jump landings.

The advantage of using a leg press exercise is the application of a weight intensity of less than body weight . Once you can perform the exercise with body weight, you can discontinue the leg press and use body-weight activities in the rehabilitation program.

Rectus femoris

Vastus medialis

Semimembranosus

Semitendinosus

Gastrocnemius

Soleus

Vastus lateralis

Gluteus medius

Gluteus maximus

Biceps femoris

Execution

1. Stand erect with the feet approximately shoulder-width apart and the toes turned out slightly. Extend the arms in front of the body or place the hands on the hips.
2. Slowly lower the body by extending the hips and bending the knees until the thighs are slightly below parallel to the floor. If you feel pain during the descent, stop just above the point of pain.
3. Return to starting position.
4. Perform the prescribed number of repetitions.

Muscles Involved

Primary: Quadriceps (rectus femoris, vastus lateralis, vastus medialis, vastus intermedius), hamstrings (semitendinosus, semimembranosus, biceps femoris), gluteus maximus

Secondary: Gluteus medius, gluteus minimus, erector spinae (iliocostalis, longissimus, spinalis), gastrocnemius, soleus

Basketball Focus

Most basketball activities, such as the jump shot, begin and end on two feet. This exercise restores both strength and stability and establishes a baseline of strength to which higher loads may be added over time. During the exercise, do not shift your body weight away from the injured leg and place more weight on your healthy leg. After gaining proficiency in this exercise, progress to the back or front squat (see chapter 2).

Execution

1. Stand on a plyometric box. The height of the box depends on the severity of the knee condition. Begin with a 4-inch (10 cm) box and progress in height until you can perform 3 sets of 10 repetitions from an 8-inch (20 cm) box.

2. Step down from the box slowly with the healthy leg while dorsiflexing the ankle. Make floor contact with the heel. Maintain control of your knee; do not allow it to turn inward (valgus) or outward (varus). The injured leg stays on the box.

3. Return to starting position.

4. Perform the prescribed number of repetitions and switch legs.

Muscles Involved

Primary: Quadriceps (rectus femoris, vastus lateralis, vastus medialis, vastus intermedius), hamstrings (semitendinosus, semimembranosus, biceps femoris), gluteus medius

Secondary: Gluteus maximus, gastrocnemius, soleus, rectus abdominis, transversus abdominis, internal oblique, external oblique

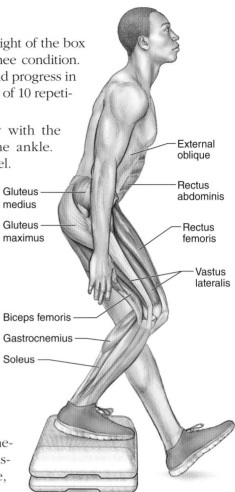

External oblique

Rectus abdominis

Rectus femoris

Vastus lateralis

Gluteus medius

Gluteus maximus

Biceps femoris

Gastrocnemius

Soleus

Basketball Focus

This exercise enhances eccentric strength and emphasizes the quadriceps. It also is used sometimes to determine readiness to initiate running activities when returning from injury.

Execution

1. Stand erect facing a box. Start with a 12-inch (30 cm) box and gradually increase the height.

2. Lower your body into a squat by extending your hips and bending your knees.

3. Reverse direction and jump vertically as high as possible. Land softly on top of the box.

4. Perform the prescribed number of box jumps.

Muscles Involved

Primary: Quadriceps (rectus femoris, vastus lateralis, vastus medialis, vastus intermedius), hamstrings (semitendinosus, semimembranosus, biceps femoris), gluteus maximus, gluteus medius, gastrocnemius

Secondary: Rectus abdominis, transversus abdominis, gluteus minimus, soleus

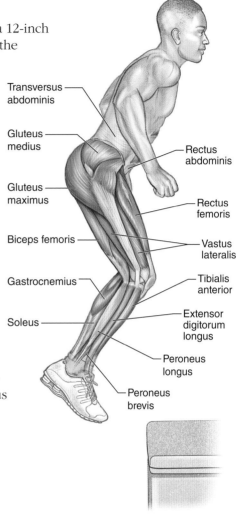

Transversus abdominis
Gluteus medius
Gluteus maximus
Biceps femoris
Gastrocnemius
Soleus
Rectus abdominis
Rectus femoris
Vastus lateralis
Tibialis anterior
Extensor digitorum longus
Peroneus longus
Peroneus brevis

Basketball Focus

Vertical jumping onto a box allows you to output a high level of power but lowers the impact forces placed on the lower extremities when compared to jumping and landing in place. This exercise restores your ability to explode while on the basketball court, whether accelerating, jumping for a rebound, or shooting the ball.

SCAPULAR DYSKINESIS

The shoulder is made up of three joints and one articulation. The three joints of the shoulder are the sternoclavicular (SC) joint, acromioclavicular (AC) joint, and glenohumeral (GH) joint. The scapulothoracic articulation is the connection between the scapula (shoulder blade) and thoracic spine (upper back). The SC joint is the only connection to the skeleton. It connects the clavicle (collarbone) to the sternum. The AC joint connects the clavicle to the acromion and has multiple ligaments for static stability of the shoulder complex. The GH joint is the ball-and-socket joint of the shoulder. This joint is made of ligaments for static stability and rotator cuff muscles (supraspinatus, infraspinatus, teres minor, subscapularis) for dynamic stability of the shoulder complex. The scapulothoracic articulation is important in the stability of the shoulder complex. It has major muscle attachments that connect the scapula to the thoracic spine.

The thoracic spine (upper back) has 12 segments (T1 to T12). These segments have muscle attachments and move when the muscles are used. For example, when you lift your arm, the muscles and thoracic spine move to complete the task. The thoracic spine has the potential for multiplanar movement (flexing and extending, side bending, and rotating). Basketball players have a tendency to lose thoracic spine extension and rotation toward the nondominant side (so a right-handed shooter will lose rotation to the left) as a result of repetitive shooting and trained movement patterns.

Competitive athletes in overhead sports typically try to maximize the overall effort of the upper extremity when throwing to maximize the overall velocity of the object thrown. The art of shooting, rebounding, and defending in basketball requires explosive full-body movements completed with proper timing, coordination, flexibility, and strength of the upper and lower extremities and trunk. It is believed that the complex motion of the thoracic spine contributes to an effective shooting motion. Unfortunately, the thoracic spine is susceptible to motion restrictions that potentially limit its contribution to an optimal shooting of the ball. Therefore, it is thought that thoracic spine mobility will help in restoring the total arc of motion at the GH joint and help maintain the anatomic positioning of the scapula on the thorax.

The scapula and shoulder joint must work together to produce pain-free and powerful shoulder range of motion. This is called scapulohumeral rhythm and has three phases. These phases restore normal anatomical positioning and motion at the shoulder complex.

Phase 1: As the humerus is elevated to 30 degrees, the scapula is known to be in the setting phase. During this phase, there is minimal movement of the scapula.

Phase 2: As the humerus elevates from 30 to 90 degrees of abduction, the scapula must move and rotate. During this phase, there is a 2:1 ratio of humerus mobility to scapular mobility.

Phase 3: As the humerus elevates the last 90 degrees of shoulder abduction, the scapula must rotate and upwardly elevate. During the final phase, there is a 2:1 ratio of humerus mobility to scapular mobility.

This results in a total shoulder elevation of 180 degrees in which 120 degrees is due to humeral elevation and 60 degrees is due to scapula rotation. As you actively complete the range of motion in shoulder abduction, a coach or trainer should see not only the quality of the active motion but also your static positioning of the scapula on the thorax.

Alterations in static and dynamic scapula positioning occur in athletes with shoulder pathology. Due to the intimate nature of the scapula's articulation with the thoracic spine and the coupling motion of the scapulohumeral joint, atypical positioning or loss of scapula control is called scapula dyskinesis (Yin et al. 2014).

Normal scapular positioning is observed from the posterior view. The position of each scapula appears identical in height and distance off the thoracic spine. On average, each scapula measures 2 to 3 inches (5-7.5 cm) off the center of the spine. It should appear flat on the thorax. In most athletes, the dominant arm will have abnormal positioning of the scapula. It will measure greater than 3 inches off the spine, appear lower in comparison to the other scapula, and exhibit a winged (tilted) position.

This abnormal static positioning of the scapula may be due to bony deformities of the thoracic spine, which are present at birth. For example, too much or too little of thoracic spine kyphosis (the curvature of the spine) can result in abnormal positioning of the scapula. Injuries to any of the anatomical structures of the shoulder, muscle imbalances, or loss of muscle flexibility may also contribute to abnormal scapular positioning. This abnormal positioning will result in abnormal motion, which disrupts scapulohumeral rhythm.

Although bony deformities cannot be changed, you can address muscle imbalances and muscle flexibility about the shoulder complex. Restoring muscle balance and flexibility reduces the risk of injury and may restore more optimal scapular positioning, which will normalize scapulohumeral rhythm and enhance performance.

Regarding the shoulder complex, the scapular stabilizers are the most important muscles. These muscles connect the scapulae to the thoracic spine and are the anchors that facilitate proper scapular setting and restore normal scapulohumeral rhythm. Muscle activation and coordination of firing patterns result in force couples for scapular control. The most important force couples are the upper and lower trapezius and the rhomboids and serratus anterior muscles. The lower trapezius is the most important stabilizer; it maintains scapular control during shoulder elevation. The lower trapezius must be strong and you must be able to exercise control and isolate this muscle during strengthening. The lower trapezius is prone to weakness due to the dominance of the upper trapezius.

In addition to restoring strength and muscle firing patterns, restoring muscle and joint flexibility is important for normalizing static and dynamic scapular positioning. Scapular winging (tilting) may be the result of a tight muscle or joint. Basketball players tend to have tightness in the pectoralis and latissimus dorsi muscles, which results in anterior tilting of the scapula. Because of repetitive overhead motions, players lose internal rotation of the glenohumeral joint. This may be due to tightness in the posterior capsule of the shoulder or tightness in the joint capsule. If total arc of motion is not restored, the result is excessive distance (more than 3 inches) between the spine and scapula.

When addressing scapular dyskinesis in basketball players, the primary focus should be to restore shoulder flexibility and mobility and total arc of motion. Shoulder range of motion can be restored via stretching or soft tissue massage to the surrounding muscle groups (upper trapezius, posterior capsule, latissimus dorsi, and pectoralis) and encouraging thoracic spine mobility.

While restoring range of motion, progress to strengthening the scapular stabilizers and rotator cuff muscles. Isotonic strengthening progresses to plyometric strength training to increase power. Muscle strength and power and the restoration of proper muscle firing patterns (scapular stabilizers fire before rotator cuff muscles) are imperative for preventing shoulder injuries and are the foundation for enhancing performance.

Following are the stretching, range-of-motion, and strengthening exercises in this chapter:

Shoulder Stretching

Posterior capsule stretch

Latissimus dorsi stretch

Pectoralis stretch

Sleeper stretch

Shoulder Range of Motion

Thoracic spine mobility

Shoulder Isotonic Strengthening

YTW

Side-lying shoulder external rotation

Cheerleader

Overhead press

Shoulder Plyometric Strengthening

Overhead medicine ball toss

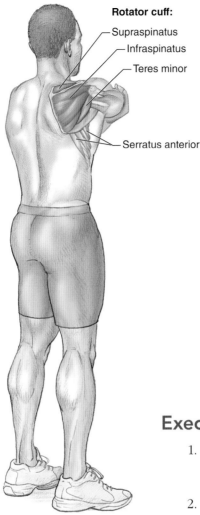

Rotator cuff:
- Supraspinatus
- Infraspinatus
- Teres minor

Serratus anterior

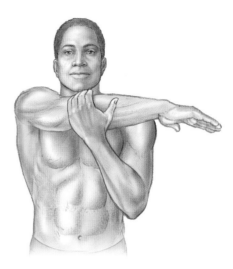

Anterior view.

Execution

1. Stand erect and pull one elbow across your body until you feel a stretch in the back of the shoulder.
2. Hold this position for 30 seconds. Do 3 to 5 times a day.
3. To advance the exercise, hold on to a pole or other stationary object and lean toward your arm.

Muscles Involved

Primary: Rotator cuff (infraspinatus, supraspinatus, subscapularis, teres minor), posterior deltoid

Secondary: Serratus anterior, latissimus dorsi

Basketball Focus

This stretch restores flexibility in the back of the shoulder to allow for increased shoulder range of motion during shooting and defending.

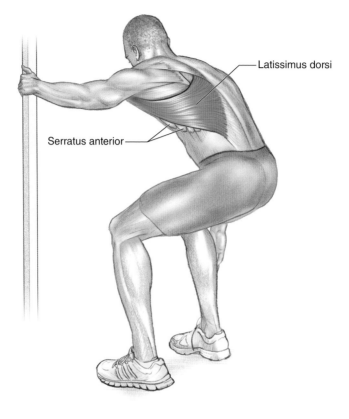

Latissimus dorsi

Serratus anterior

Execution

1. Stand and hold on to a pole or other stationary object with one hand.
2. Lean back until you feel a stretch along the border of the latissimus muscle.
3. Hold this position for 30 seconds. Do 3 to 5 times a day.

Muscles Involved

Primary: Latissimus dorsi

Secondary: Serratus anterior

Basketball Focus

This stretch restores the flexibility in the back and shoulder to increase shoulder range of motion during shooting and defending.

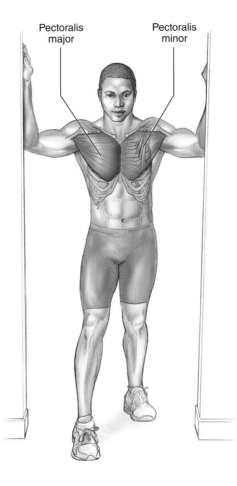

Execution

1. Stand in a corner or doorway with elbows at shoulder height. Place forearms on the walls.
2. Lean into the corner or doorway until you feel a stretch in the upper chest.
3. Hold this position for 30 seconds. Do 3 to 5 times a day.

Muscles Involved

Primary: Pectoralis major, pectoralis minor

Basketball Focus

This stretch restores flexibility in the back and shoulder to increase shoulder range of motion during shooting and defending.

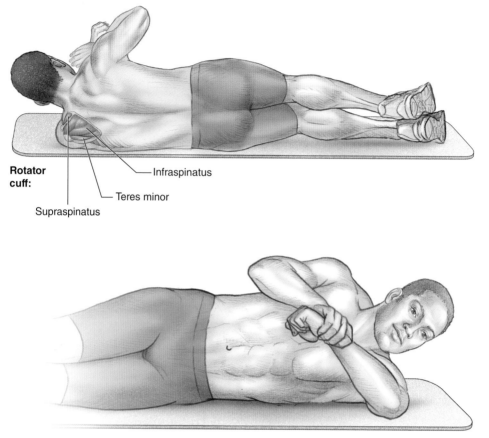

Rotator cuff:

Infraspinatus

Teres minor

Supraspinatus

Anterior view.

Execution

1. Lie on the affected shoulder as if sleeping on your side.
2. Raise the lower arm at a 90-degree angle in front of you. Bend the elbow 90 degrees so the hand is near the upper shoulder.
3. Using the upper hand, gently press the lower hand toward the floor until you feel a stretch on the posterior aspect of the shoulder.
4. Hold this position for 10 seconds. Do 10 times.

Muscles Involved

Primary: Rotator cuff (infraspinatus, supraspinatus, subscapularis, teres minor), posterior deltoid

Basketball Focus

This stretch restores the flexibility in the back and shoulder to increase shoulder range of motion during shooting and defending.

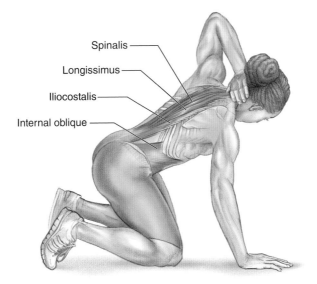

Spinalis

Longissimus

Iliocostalis

Internal oblique

Execution

1. Assume a quadruped position (on all fours). Lift one arm and place the hand behind the head.
2. Rotate toward the arm behind the head. Feel the stretch in the upper back toward the arm behind the head.
3. Hold this position for 3 to 5 seconds. Do 30 times on each side.
4. To advance the exercise, stand and hold a stick behind your back. Slightly bend both knees and flex the hips to about 75 degrees. Rotate from side to side.

Muscles Involved

Primary: Spinalis, longissimus, external oblique, internal oblique

Basketball Focus

This stretch restores the flexibility in the back and shoulder to increase shoulder range of motion during shooting and defending.

Rotator cuff:

Supraspinatus

Infraspinatus

Teres minor

Middle trapezius

Middle deltoid

Posterior deltoid

Rhomboid major

Lower trapezius

Erector spinae:

Spinalis

Longissimus

Iliocostalis

Transversus abdominis

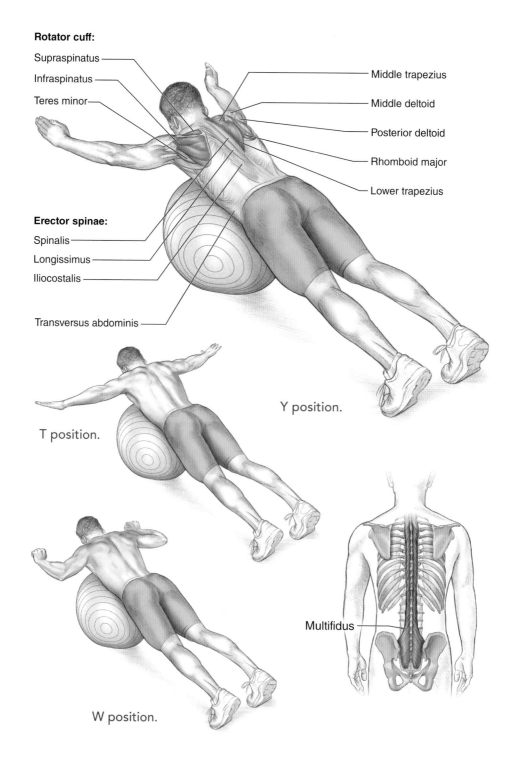

Y position.

T position.

W position.

Multifidus

Execution

1. Lie on a Physioball with your arms at your sides.
2. Pinch shoulder blades together. For the Y position, lift arms straight up toward your head; return to the starting position. For the T position, lift arms to your sides; return to starting position. For the W position, lift arms to your sides with elbows bent and rotate arms upward; return to the starting position.
3. Alternate Ys, Ts, and Ws for 3 sets of 10 repetitions.
4. To advance the exercise, add hand weights.

Muscles Involved

Primary: Middle trapezius, lower trapezius, rhomboids, rotator cuff (supraspinatus, infraspinatus, teres minor, subscapularis)

Secondary: Biceps brachii, posterior deltoid, lateral deltoid, multifidus, erector spinae (iliocostalis, longissimus, spinalis), transversus abdominis

Basketball Focus

Strengthen the scapular stabilizer muscles to facilitate proper muscle firing patterns that assist with shooting, defending, and blocking.

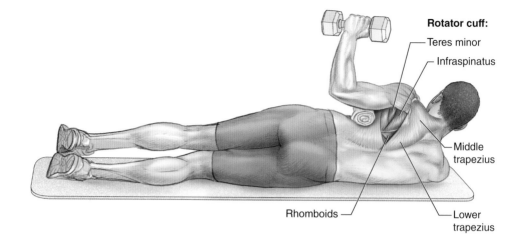

Rotator cuff:
Teres minor
Infraspinatus
Middle trapezius
Rhomboids
Lower trapezius

Execution

1. Lie on your side with a rolled towel under your arm and your elbow bent to 90 degrees.
2. Pinch your shoulder blades together and lift your forearm toward the ceiling. Keep the elbow bent and rotate through the shoulder.
3. Complete 3 sets of 10 repetitions.
4. To advance the exercise, add hand weights.

Muscles Involved

Primary: Rotator cuff (infraspinatus, teres minor)

Secondary: Middle trapezius, lower trapezius, rhomboids

Basketball Focus

Strengthening the rotator cuff muscles will assist with shooting, defending, and blocking.

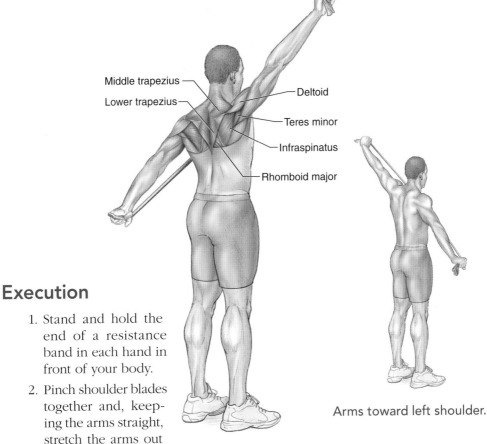

Middle trapezius
Lower trapezius
Deltoid
Teres minor
Infraspinatus
Rhomboid major

Arms toward left shoulder.

Execution

1. Stand and hold the end of a resistance band in each hand in front of your body.
2. Pinch shoulder blades together and, keeping the arms straight, stretch the arms out to the sides. Return to the starting position.
3. Stretch arms up and toward the right shoulder. Return to the starting position.
4. Stretch arms out to the sides. Return to the starting position.
5. Stretch arms up and toward the left. Return to the starting position.
6. Perform the cheerleader pattern for 3 sets of 5 repetitions.
7. To advance the exercise, use a stronger resistance band.

Muscles Involved

Primary: Middle trapezius, lower trapezius, rhomboids, rotator cuff (supraspinatus, infraspinatus, teres minor, subscapularis)

Secondary: Biceps brachii, anterior deltoid, posterior deltoid, lateral deltoid

Basketball Focus

Strengthen the scapular stabilizer muscles to facilitate proper muscle firing patterns that assist with shooting, defending, and blocking.

Deeper muscles

More superficial muscles

Anterior deltoid

Lateral deltoid

Supraspinatus

Middle trapezius

Lower trapezius

Rhomboid minor

Rhomboid major

Execution

1. Stand holding a barbell or dumbbells. Elbows are bent at 30-degree angles.

2. Hold weights at shoulder level. Lift the weights by raising the arms overhead to a fully extended position. The path of the weights should go directly overhead, concluding with both arms in line with the ears. Do not arch the back or look up.

3. Slowly lower weights to the starting position.

4. Perform 3 sets of 10 repetitions.

5. To advance the exercise, increase the weight.

Muscles Involved

Primary: Rotator cuff muscles (supraspinatus)

Secondary: Anterior deltoid, lateral deltoid, middle trapezius, lower trapezius, rhomboids, rectus abdominis

Basketball Focus

Strengthening the rotator cuff muscles will increase general shoulder strength, leading to improvement in shooting, defending, and blocking.

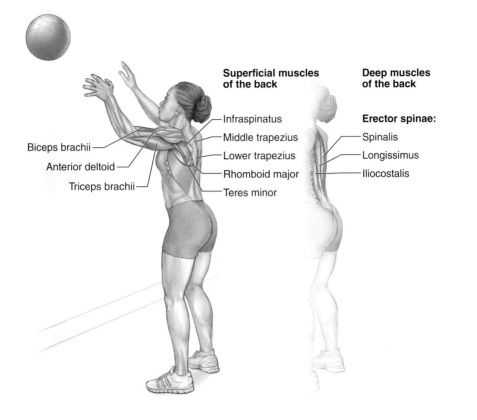

Superficial muscles of the back

- Infraspinatus
- Middle trapezius
- Lower trapezius
- Rhomboid major
- Teres minor

Biceps brachii
Anterior deltoid
Triceps brachii

Deep muscles of the back

Erector spinae:
- Spinalis
- Longissimus
- Iliocostalis

Execution

1. Stand a few inches away from a wall. Hold a medicine ball overhead with the arms bent to 90 degrees.
2. Toss the ball repetitively against the wall, mimicking the action of a soccer throw-in, for 10-second intervals.
3. Perform the prescribed number of throws.
4. To advance the exercise, use a heavier medicine ball or increase the timed intervals.

Muscles Involved

Primary: Biceps brachii, triceps brachii, rotator cuff (supraspinatus, infraspinatus, teres minor, subscapularis)

Secondary: Anterior deltoid, middle trapezius, lower trapezius, rhomboids, multifidus, erector spinae (iliocostalis, longissimus, spinalis), transversus abdominis, rectus abdominis

Basketball Focus

Plyometric strengthening will increase power and help with shooting and rebounding.

chapter 9

INJURY PREVENTION FOR AVOIDING THE BENCH

The best way to treat an injury is to never get injured in the first place. Basketball players want to be on the court, not on the bench. Smart conditioning and training help to prevent chronic injuries caused by overuse, repetitive motion, and overtraining. This translates to three-point shots without shoulder pain and fast breaks without limping.

The two most important joints in the body related to basketball performance are the knee and the shoulder. Although anterior cruciate ligament (ACL) injuries in the NBA make up just over 13 percent of all basketball injuries, they are among the most debilitating injuries, followed by injuries to the shoulder complex. Knees play a key role in basketball success because they are involved in nearly every movement, including jumping for a rebound, running up the court, and changing direction. The shoulders come into play in all shooting, blocking, and rebounding motions. Overuse injuries of the shoulder are common because of frequent overhead motions.

In this chapter, we cover key ways to prevent injuries to these areas (prehabilitation, if you will), beginning with the knees.

PREVENTING ACL INJURIES

ACL prevention programs have received much attention over the past several years due in no small part to how common ACL injuries have become and their devastating effects.

A ligament is made of strong fibrous connective tissue and provides stability between two bones. In the case of the ACL (figure 9.1), it connects from the medial aspect of the lateral femoral condyle to the anterior medial aspect of the tibial spine on the tibial plateau. The function of the ACL is to limit internal rotation and forward translation of the tibia in relation to the femur.

Basketball has the highest rate of ACL tears of any sport (Prodromos et al. 2007). Female players are four to six times more likely than male players to sustain ACL injuries, and high school athletes seem even more susceptible compared to college and professional basketball players. Additionally, the devastating effects of an ACL tear warrant significant attention. Consider the short-term effects of pain, limited function, the difficult decision to undergo surgical reconstruction, and the intense rehabilitation necessary for a comeback, not to mention missing at least one full season of competition. Roughly 23 percent of all people who have had an ACL tear will have a second ACL injury. The long-term effects may be even worse. Several studies indicate a 100 percent chance of developing osteoarthritis of the knee within 20 years of injury, regardless of whether or not the athlete undergoes reconstruction. That means a 15-year-old female player who tears her ACL will have clinically significant knee arthritis before or at 35 years of age plus a one in four chance of a retear or of injuring the ACL in her other knee. Prevention is the best method of treatment for the ACL.

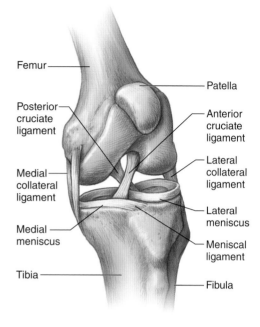

Figure 9.1   Knee ligaments and tissues.

The question of whether an ACL injury can be prevented is hotly debated in the literature. Sadly, there is no such thing as a 100 percent guarantee for any program. It might be a matter of semantics, but you should think of this as injury reduction rather than prevention. The truth is you simply cannot prevent all tears, but you can help reduce the number. You are unlikely to prevent an ACL tear from direct trauma; however, the majority of ACL tears are noncontact injuries, meaning that injuries are related more to how an athlete moves when playing basketball. It stands to reason that if you can train to move properly and strengthen the muscles involved in controlling efficient movement patterns, then you can reduce the likelihood of the injury.

ACL injuries most often occur as a result of the combination of three motions: increased tibial external rotation, increased hip internal rotation and adduction, and dynamic knee valgus. Any one of these motions in isolation typically would not injure the ACL, but in combination, the stress placed on the ligament is simply too much.

Let's take a closer look at the concept known as dynamic valgus. The word *valgus* describes a knock-knee position; conversely, *varus* describes a bow-legged position. Dynamic valgus occurs when the athlete's knee comes inward excessively while performing a physical activity, such as landing from a rebound. This valgus movement places unnatural forces on the ACL, making it susceptible to a sprain. This scenario usually occurs when landing from a jump, pivoting, or cutting. In specific regard to cutting, it is common for these high stresses to occur when an athlete decelerates from running in an effort to rapidly change direction. This is especially true when any of these actions are not anticipated, which frequently occurs in basketball. For example, a player who is driving toward the basket attempts to outmaneuver another player. At the very moment of deceleration, if the player's trunk, hip, and leg muscles are not strong enough to maintain optimal alignment, the player's leg collapses into this position of danger (dynamic valgus), thus exposing the ligament to injury. This can and usually happens in a split second.

Thanks to the great work done at Cincinnati Children's Hospital by researchers Timothy Hewett, Gregory Myer, and Kevin Ford, ACL prevention training programs have advanced to what they are today (Myer et al. 2008; Myer, Ford, and Hewett 2004, 2008). These researchers speak about neuromuscular imbalance patterns that predispose athletes to ACL injury and how to identify and best train to correct them. Four neuromuscular imbalance patterns have been identified: ligament dominance, quadriceps dominance, leg dominance, and trunk dominance. In a full-fledged ACL prevention program, the training process is much more extensive and requires critical feedback from a qualified professional. The exercises and drills are progressive and advance based on the individual needs of the athlete. Exercises progress from more stationary strength exercises to more dynamic exercises in which power and technique are emphasized to best prepare the athlete for the stresses and demands of the sport. There is no one-size-fits-all program. Professional Athletic Performance Center in Garden City, New York, has a program that bridges the gap between where traditional physical therapy ends and sport performance training begins. In the following section are a few foundational strength exercises that address each of the neuromuscular imbalance patterns.

ACL: Ligament Dominance

Band squat
Band defensive slide
Side-lying clam

ACL: Quadriceps Dominance

Physioball hamstring curl
Russian hamstring curl

ACL: Leg Dominance

Single-leg squat off box
Bulgarian split squat

ACL: Trunk Dominance

BOSU round double crunch
Physioball lateral crunch

Neuromuscular Imbalance Pattern I: Ligament Dominance

The ligament dominance pattern, or the dynamic valgus, is the knock-knee position. To avoid this dangerous movement pattern, you need to strengthen your lateral hip muscles. Following are three exercises addressing ligament dominance.

BAND SQUAT

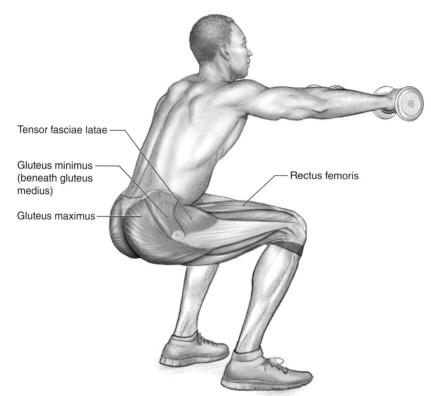

Tensor fasciae latae

Gluteus minimus
(beneath gluteus
medius)

Gluteus maximus

Rectus femoris

Execution

1. Place an elastic band just below both knees. Base the resistance on your ability to maintain both legs shoulder-width apart and knees in good alignment.

2. Perform a squat until the thighs are parallel to the floor. While in the bottom position of the squat, continue to apply outward tension to the band, activating the gluteus medius and gluteus minimus.

Muscles Involved

Primary: Quadriceps (rectus femoris, vastus lateralis, vastus medialis, vastus intermedius), gluteus medius, gluteus minimus

Secondary: Tensor fasciae latae, hamstrings (semitendinosus, biceps femoris, semimembranosus)

Basketball Focus

The band squat develops hip strength for stabilizing yourself when cutting and changing direction. If you are a beginner, start with the lightest resistance band and progress to more resistance as strength develops. As with performing squats, proper foot position and attention to knee placement are important in this exercise.

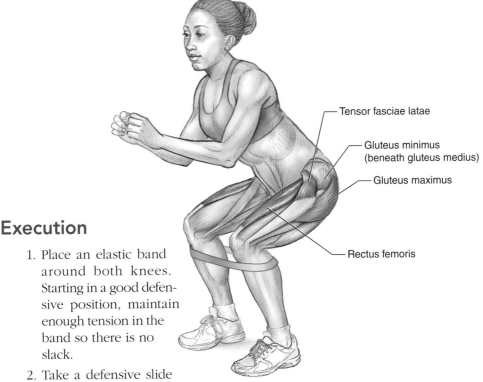

Tensor fasciae latae

Gluteus minimus
(beneath gluteus medius)

Gluteus maximus

Rectus femoris

Execution

1. Place an elastic band around both knees. Starting in a good defensive position, maintain enough tension in the band so there is no slack.

2. Take a defensive slide with one leg, increasing the tension on the band. Once you reach maximum tension based on your strength level, bring the other leg over to return to a good defensive position.

3. Perform this pattern for the required distance or repetitions.

4. Repeat the procedure moving in the other direction.

Muscles Involved

Primary: Quadriceps (rectus femoris, vastus lateralis, vastus medialis, vastus intermedius), gluteus medius, gluteus minimus

Secondary: Tensor fasciae latae, hamstrings (semitendinosus, biceps femoris, semimembranosus)

Basketball Focus

This exercise mimics a defensive slide performed in basketball. You can perform this exercise while holding your arms out as if you were defending against an opponent. As stated in the band squat exercise, this exercise helps to develop strength in the hips. Strength in the hips and gluteals is important, especially for female basketball players, in stabilizing the lower leg when pivoting and cutting.

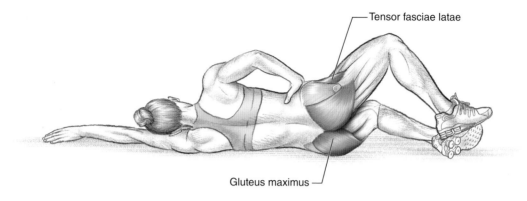

Tensor fasciae latae

Gluteus maximus

Execution

1. Place an elastic band just above both knees. Lie on your side with knees and hips flexed to about 90 degrees. The head, shoulder, knee, and ankle should be in a straight line.

2. While maintaining a good side-lying position, separate the knees and rotate the top leg out, creating tension in the band. Return to the starting position.

3. Perform the prescribed number of repetitions and switch sides.

Muscles Involved

Primary: Gluteus medius, gluteus minimus, tensor fasciae latae, piriformis, obturator externus, quadratus femoris

Secondary: Sartorius

Basketball Focus

This exercise develops gluteal and hip strength. When performing this exercise, avoid excessive rotation of the upper body. Maintain a straight line from head to shoulders, knees, and ankles. As you rotate the top leg, the feet do not come apart; all the motion is at the hip.

Neuromuscular Imbalance Pattern II: Quadriceps Dominance

In quadriceps dominance, the quadriceps muscle group overpowers the hamstring muscle group. It is difficult to accurately assess this imbalance without objective data such as an expensive isokinetic test, but the trained eye of a coach can identify this when you land with stiff knees. When you do not attain deep knee flexion, the coach can correctly assume it is due to underlying hamstring weakness and an overreliance on quadriceps muscle strength. This imbalance doesn't give the hamstrings a chance to attenuate force. To correct this pattern, pay attention to the entire posterior chain (hamstrings, glutes, and low back) to better absorb forces from landing during a jump. Following are two hamstring exercises that address quadriceps dominance.

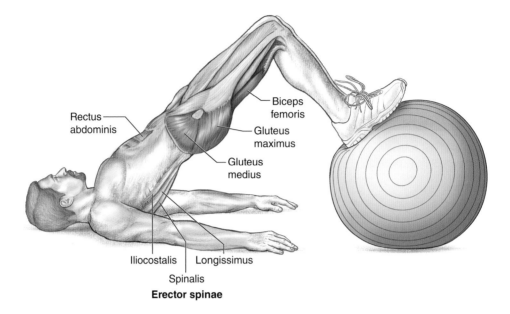

Rectus abdominis

Biceps femoris

Gluteus maximus

Gluteus medius

Iliocostalis

Longissimus

Spinalis

Erector spinae

Execution

1. Lie on your back with both feet on a Physioball, legs straight.
2. Perform a bridge by raising the hips off the floor.
3. While holding the bridge position, bend both knees and roll the ball toward the buttocks and then back out. Lower to the starting position.
4. Perform the prescribed number of repetitions.

Muscles Involved

Primary: Hamstrings (biceps femoris, semimembranosus, semitendinosus), gluteus maximus, gluteus medius, gluteus minimus

Secondary: Erector spinae (iliocostalis, longissimus, spinalis), rectus abdominis

Basketball Focus

One of the most significant injuries you could sustain during the season is a hamstring strain. Hamstring strains can last for months if not rehabbed properly and can linger. Physioball hamstring curls develop strength in the hamstrings as well as increase low back and abdominal strength during the bridging motion. Female basketball players require more posterior strength because many are quadriceps dominant when landing and cutting. Increasing hamstring strength can help protect the knees during these types of movements.

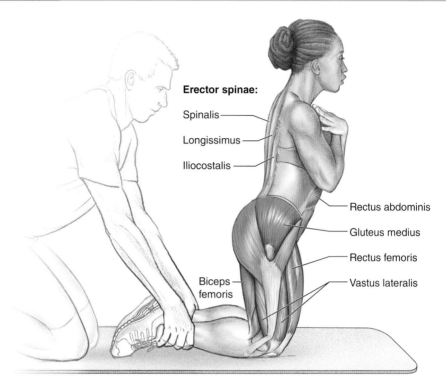

Erector spinae:

Spinalis

Longissimus

Iliocostalis

Rectus abdominis

Gluteus medius

Rectus femoris

Biceps femoris

Vastus lateralis

Execution

1. Kneel on both knees and have a partner stabilize both ankles. Place your arms at your sides with the elbows bent and arms crossed.
2. Extend at the knees while keeping a neutral spine. Lower as far as you can.
3. Once you reach optimal distance without flexing at the hips, return to the starting position using the hamstrings.
4. Perform the prescribed number of repetitions.

Muscles Involved

Primary: Hamstrings (biceps femoris, semimembranosus, semitendinosus), gluteus medius, gluteus minimus

Secondary: Erector spinae (iliocostalis, longissimus, spinalis), rectus abdominis

Basketball Focus

This exercise is a more advanced hamstring strengthening exercise that requires a partner. You can use this exercise as a supplement during a workout session. Because of the amount of running on the court during the game, limited hamstring strength puts you at a higher risk of injury.

Neuromuscular Imbalance Pattern III: Leg Dominance

Leg dominance is related to asymmetrical strength—that is, one leg is stronger than the other. This can exist naturally if you favor one leg over another, similar to hand dominance. Also, this can happen if you come back from an injury but never fully achieve pre-injury strength. The key to correcting this pattern is to perform bilateral strength movements, such as squats, and progressively train using single-leg exercises such as lunges and step-ups. To address leg dominance in our strength training programs, we typically dedicate one-third of our leg exercises to unilateral work. Here are two excellent single-leg exercises.

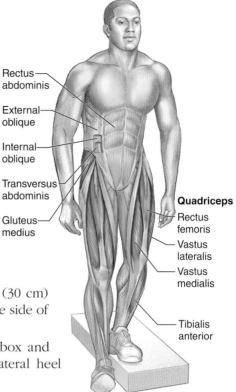

Rectus abdominis

External oblique

Internal oblique

Transversus abdominis

Gluteus medius

Quadriceps
Rectus femoris
Vastus lateralis
Vastus medialis

Tibialis anterior

Execution

1. Balance on one leg on a 12-inch (30 cm) box. The contralateral leg is off the side of the box with the foot dorsiflexed.
2. Flex the knee of the leg on the box and slowly descend until the contralateral heel makes contact with the floor.
3. Once the heel touches the floor, ascend up to the starting position.
4. Perform the prescribed number of repetitions and switch legs.

Muscles Involved

Primary: Gluteus maximus, gluteus medius, gluteus minimus, quadriceps (rectus femoris, vastus lateralis, vastus intermedius, vastus medialis), semimembranosus, semitendinosus, tibialis anterior

Secondary: Erector spinae (iliocostalis, longissimus, spinalis), transversus abdominis, rectus abdominis, internal oblique, external oblique

Basketball Focus

The single-leg squat off box requires both strength and balance. If you are new to this exercise and if balance is a problem, hold on to something sturdy. This exercise develops strength and stability in the weaker leg. Focus on proper technique when performing this exercise. You will notice a difference in strength from one side to the other, especially if you push off more on your dominant side when driving to the basket or doing a layup.

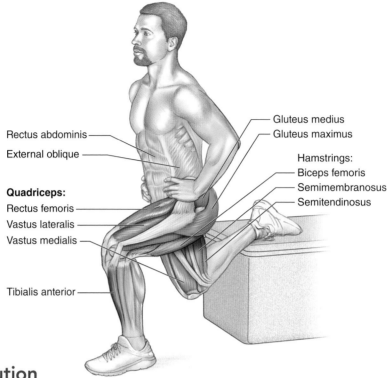

Rectus abdominis

External oblique

Quadriceps:

Rectus femoris

Vastus lateralis

Vastus medialis

Tibialis anterior

Gluteus medius

Gluteus maximus

Hamstrings:

Biceps femoris

Semimembranosus

Semitendinosus

Execution

1. Start in a lunge position with full support on the front leg and the opposite leg resting on a bench or box behind you. You can perform this exercise with a weighted bar across your shoulders.

2. Descend to 90 degrees of knee flexion on the front leg. Lunge your front leg out far enough so that your knee does not cross over your ankle.

3. Perform the prescribed number of repetitions and switch legs.

Muscles Involved

Primary: Gluteus maximus, gluteus medius, gluteus minimus, quadriceps (rectus femoris, vastus lateralis, vastus intermedius, vastus medialis), semimembranosus, semitendinosus, tibialis anterior

Secondary: Erector spinae (iliocostalis, longissimus, spinalis), transversus abdominis, rectus abdominis, internal oblique, external oblique

Basketball Focus

Like the single-leg squat, the Bulgarian split squat is an advanced exercise. This exercise requires more trunk stability than the single-leg squat because the rear foot is on a box or bench. You will discover that one side is stronger than the other, so remember to maintain strict form on your weaker side. Single-leg strength helps you generate more force into the floor when jumping off one leg. It also helps when landing from a rebound.

Neuromuscular Imbalance Pattern IV: Trunk Dominance

Trunk dominance is also known as a weak core. This pattern is apparent when you cannot demonstrate control over your body and the center of gravity is not maintained over your base of support. This is correctable by strengthening the trunk muscles and developing higher levels of proprioception (body awareness). Following are two exercises that address trunk dominance.

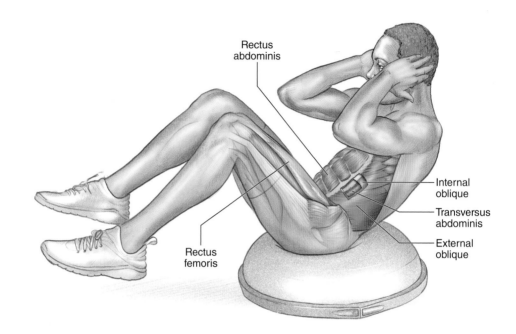

Rectus abdominis

Internal oblique

Transversus abdominis

External oblique

Rectus femoris

Execution

1. Sit balanced on the round side of the BOSU.
2. Flex your trunk simultaneously with hip flexion. Bend the knees and the elbows and place hands by the ears.
3. Perform the prescribed number of repetitions.

Muscles Involved

Primary: Rectus abdominis, transversus abdominis, internal oblique, external oblique

Secondary: Erector spinae (iliocostalis, longissimus, spinalis), rectus femoris, iliopsoas

Basketball Focus

A strong core is required for all athletic movements—running, jumping, and defending. Maintaining a strong core will help you stand your ground when an opponent charges into you. The trunk muscles stabilize your center of gravity when changing direction or landing from a jump. When you cut and plant your leg, momentum will continue unless you have the trunk strength to stop that momentum. If you do not have that trunk strength, you will be at a higher risk of knee injury.

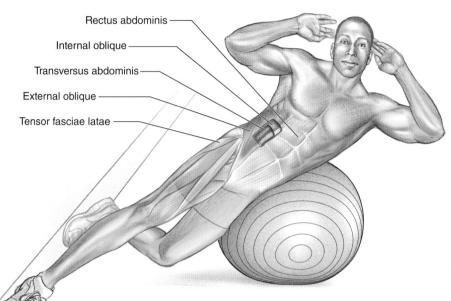

Rectus abdominis
Internal oblique
Transversus abdominis
External oblique
Tensor fasciae latae

Execution

1. Place a Physioball beside your hips and lean into it on your side. Cross one leg in front of the other and place your feet against a wall to stabilize your lower body.

2. Maintain a straight body alignment from the shoulders to the hips, knees, and ankles. Laterally flex the upper body over the Physioball and then return to the starting position. Hold a weighted ball overhead to progress the exercise and make it more challenging.

3. Perform the prescribed number of repetitions and switch sides.

Muscles Involved

Primary: Internal oblique, external oblique, transversus abdominis

Secondary: Erector spinae (iliocostalis, longissimus, spinalis), rectus abdominis, tensor fasciae latae

Basketball Focus

Like the BOSU round double crunch, the Physioball lateral crunch develops the side musculature required for rotation and lateral flexion. Because you move in multiple planes, all areas of the trunk need to be strong. When you jump and fight for a rebound, your upper body may move in an awkward position. A strong core helps to stabilize the upper body so you reduce the amount of stress on your knees when you land from a jump.

PREVENTING SHOULDER INJURIES

The term *scapular dyskinesis* was coined by Dr. J.P. Warner (1992), who found this condition in 64 percent of his patients with glenohumeral instability and in nearly 100 percent of patients with rotator cuff impingement. This condition is also known as a SICK scapula: **s**capular malposition, **i**nferior medial border prominence, **c**oracoid pain and malposition, and dys**k**inesis of scapular movement. It describes the abnormal movement of the scapula (shoulder blade) during activity. This syndrome usually occurs in athletes in overhead-type sports, such as throwers and basketball players, and is usually characterized by an abnormal positioning of the scapula, such as drooping or winging.

Scapular dyskinesis is thought to contribute to the development of shoulder injuries such as impingement. Although it may appear that the affected shoulder has a lower position than the opposite shoulder, the reality is that the affected scapula is malpositioned; often it tilts forward and is protracted. This malpositioning of the scapula may be a detriment to the shoulder complex during arm raises overhead.

The glenohumeral (ball and socket) and scapulothoracic (scapula resting on the rib cage) joints of the shoulder go through a specific sequence of overhead motion. In a normal shoulder, the two joints show a specific relationship during overhead movements in the sagittal and coronal planes. At the initiation of arm elevation, the first 30 degrees is described as the setting phase of motion. From 30 to 90 degrees of arm elevation, for every 2 degrees of arm elevation there is 1 degree of scapular upward rotation. As the arm continues overhead from 90 to 180 degrees of overhead motion, this ratio adjusts to 1:1. Therefore, the arm elevates 120 degrees as the scapula rotates 60 degrees, resulting in a total shoulder range of motion of 180 degrees as the arm moves overhead.

This cooperative sequence of overhead motion is essential. During overhead motion, it is important for the head of the humerus (the ball in the ball-and-socket joint) to maintain its position in the center of the glenoid (the socket). Since the glenoid is part of the scapula, proper positioning of the scapula during overhead motion is critical. Deviation of the scapula, or scapular dyskinesis, during this range-of-motion process could result in a shoulder injury, especially if the motion is repetitive as in basketball. Prevention of this condition is important not only for continued injury-free play throughout the season, but for optimal basketball performance as well.

Three common causes of scapular dyskinesis and possible shoulder pathology are muscle and posterior capsule tightness, muscle weakness, and muscle fatigue. The tightness that commonly occurs with scapular dyskinesis usually is observed in the pectoralis minor, which can result in an anterior tilt of the scapula and the posterior capsule of the shoulder; this may result in glenohumeral internal rotation deficit (GIRD). GIRD creates an obligatory anterior and superior translation of the humeral head with associated loss of shoulder internal rotation.

Common muscle weakness at the scapula occurs at the serratus anterior, lower and middle trapezius, and rhomboids. When these muscles are weak or inhibited, they have a limited ability to produce torque and stabilize the scapula. An additional effect of weakness is abnormal firing patterns of these muscles, resulting in poor scapular mechanics and positioning.

Muscle fatigue may also affect glenohumeral motion as documented in a classic research study by Dr. T.L. Wickiewicz (Chen et al. 1999). Shoulder muscle fatigue was demonstrated to result in the superior migration of the head of the humerus from the normal position at the midglenoid, resulting in the narrowing of the subacromial space and setting the stage for possible shoulder impingement. Fatigue will also affect the position of the scapula: It may anteriorly rotate, protract, and downwardly rotate. The combination of this abnormal scapular position and the superior migration of the humerus may result in shoulder pathology. The following exercises may help prevent scapular dyskinesis and reduce the risk of shoulder pathology.

Posterior capsule (sleeper) stretch

Pectoralis stretch

Scaption

Push-up plus

Military press

Seated row

Horizontal abduction

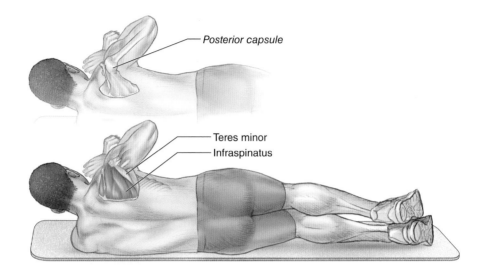

Posterior capsule

Teres minor

Infraspinatus

Execution

1. Lie on your side with your head lifted or well supported by pillows.

2. Raise the downside arm to 90 degrees and flex the elbow to 90 degrees. Bend your knees to assume a stable base.

3. Place the hand of the opposite arm just below the wrist of the affected side and slowly push (rotate) the forearm toward the floor until you feel a slight stretch. Be sure to maintain the 90-degree position at both the shoulder and elbow.

4. Maintain the stretch for 20 to 30 seconds.

5. Perform 3 to 5 repetitions. Switch sides.

Muscles Involved

Primary: Posterior capsule, infraspinatus

Secondary: Teres minor

Basketball Focus

The sleeper stretch is traditionally thought of as a baseball stretch, but it is just as useful for basketball athletes. Basketball requires repeated reaches overhead during both offense and defense. Optimal flexibility and mobility in this region can only improve shoulder function.

Execution

1. Stand erect in a doorway.
2. Raise both arms to 90 degrees (shoulder height). Flex both elbows to 90 degrees and place your forearms against the sides of the door frame.
3. Lean slightly forward through the door until you feel a slight stretch in the chest muscles.
4. Maintain this stretch for 20 to 30 seconds.
5. Perform 3 to 5 repetitions.

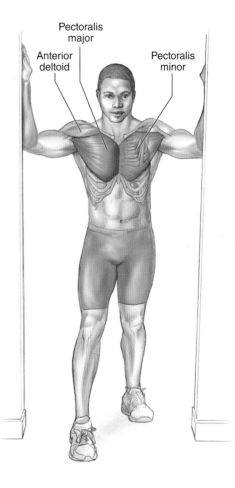

Pectoralis major

Anterior deltoid

Pectoralis minor

Muscles Involved

Primary: Pectoralis major, pectoralis minor

Secondary: Anterior deltoid

Basketball Focus

Flexible pectoralis major muscles allow you to maintain proper defensive position while your arms are raised overhead and as you reach up to block shots. If you lack flexibility in the pectorals, reaching overhead or out to the side is not efficient or effective, especially if you have long limbs.

SCAPTION

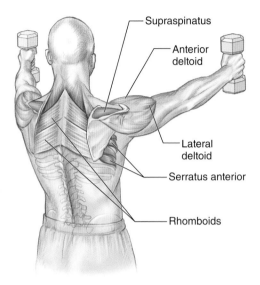

Supraspinatus

Anterior deltoid

Lateral deltoid

Serratus anterior

Rhomboids

Execution

1. Stand erect with the feet shoulder-width apart. Hold a dumbbell of a pre-scribed weight in each hand at the sides of the thighs with the thumbs pointing straight ahead.

2. Raise the arms, keeping them straight at a 45-degree angle to the body until they reach shoulder height.

3. Lower the dumbbells in a controlled manner to the starting position.

4. Perform the prescribed number of repetitions.

Muscles Involved

Primary: Serratus anterior, supraspinatus

Secondary: Anterior deltoid, lateral deltoid, rhomboids

Basketball Focus

This exercise builds the force couple at the shoulder girdle required for efficiently moving the arms overhead for shooting. It also addresses muscle imbalances that often occur when these muscles are ignored in favor of more common traditional exercises such as the bench press.

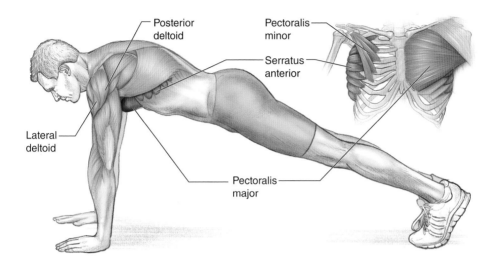

Execution

1. Lie facedown on the floor and assume a traditional push-up position with your hands shoulder-width apart, the elbows flexed with the palms on the floor, and the body fully extended.

2. While keeping the body straight, extend the arms to assume a full up position in the push-up.

3. Continue to push into the floor and extend your upper back until it is 2 to 3 inches (~5-8 cm) higher than your shoulders.

4. Lower your body to the floor to return to the starting position.

5. Perform the prescribed number of repetitions.

Muscles Involved

Primary: Serratus anterior, pectoralis major, pectoralis minor

Secondary: Anterior deltoid, lateral deltoid

Basketball Focus

The push-up plus has long been a favorite for strengthening the serratus anterior and pectoral muscle groups, which are important for passing and shooting the basketball.

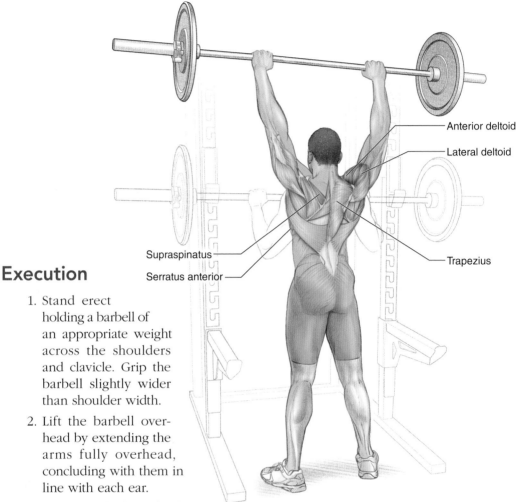

Anterior deltoid

Lateral deltoid

Trapezius

Supraspinatus

Serratus anterior

Execution

1. Stand erect holding a barbell of an appropriate weight across the shoulders and clavicle. Grip the barbell slightly wider than shoulder width.

2. Lift the barbell overhead by extending the arms fully overhead, concluding with them in line with each ear.

3. Lower the barbell slowly in a controlled manner to the starting position.

4. Perform the prescribed number of repetitions.

Muscles Involved

Primary: Serratus anterior, anterior deltoid, lateral deltoid, supraspinatus

Secondary: Subscapularis, trapezius

Basketball Focus

Strength and flexibility for overhead shooting and blocking are critical. The military press specifically addresses these needs while also helping to prevent scapular dyskinesia, which has been commonly observed in basketball players.

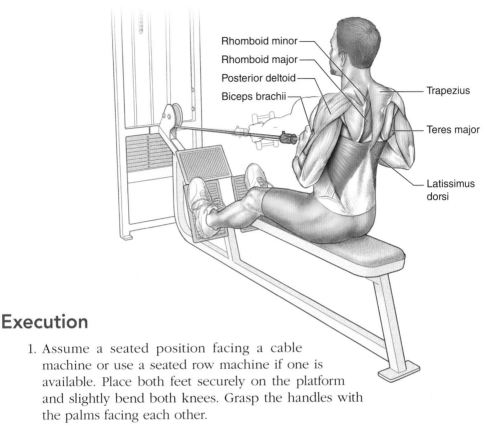

Rhomboid minor
Rhomboid major
Posterior deltoid
Biceps brachii
Trapezius
Teres major
Latissimus dorsi

Execution

1. Assume a seated position facing a cable machine or use a seated row machine if one is available. Place both feet securely on the platform and slightly bend both knees. Grasp the handles with the palms facing each other.

2. Stabilizing the muscles of the upper back, pull the handles at a controlled speed toward your lower chest while keeping your elbows at your sides. Do not let the elbows pass the sides of your body. Keep your spine erect and do not lean back.

3. Maintaining a stable torso, return the handles to the start position by extending the arms slowly and with control.

4. Perform the prescribed number of repetitions.

Muscles Involved

Primary: Latissimus dorsi, rhomboids

Secondary: Trapezius, teres major, posterior deltoid, biceps brachii

Basketball Focus

The seated row not only helps you develop musculature to prevent shoulder injuries, but it also helps you guard and secure the ball from your opponent.

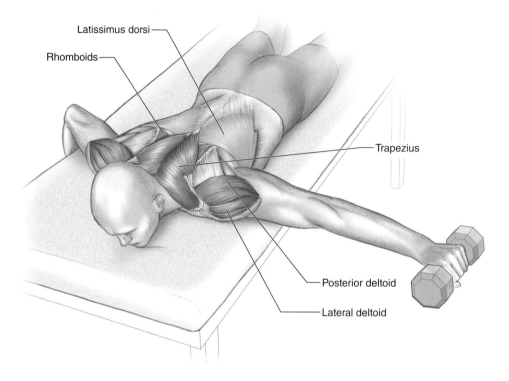

Execution

1. Lie facedown on a table or wide bench with the exercising arm hanging from the side of the table or bench. Hold a dumbbell of an appropriate weight in the hanging hand with the thumb facing forward.

2. Maintaining a firm grip on the dumbbell, raise the arm straight out to the side of the body until the arm is fully extended.

3. Slowly lower the arm to the starting position.

4. Perform the prescribed number of repetitions.

Muscles Involved

Primary: Rhomboids, trapezius, posterior deltoid, lateral deltoid

Secondary: Latissimus dorsi

Basketball Focus

This exercise helps you develop and maintain endurance in the arms, which is required at the end of the second half or fourth quarter of the game when playing aggressive offense or defense.

chapter 10

PUTTING IT ALL TOGETHER

Basketball training requires performing specific exercises, but just as important is an organized plan of action. As in other areas of life, such as saving for a child's college education, constructing a home, or establishing a retirement account, a plan of action aids in meeting goals. Each of these goals requires a plan to ensure proper application, satisfaction, and results. An athlete's training program is no different. Assessment, preparation of both athlete and program, selection of exercises, and order of exercises are detailed in this chapter.

EVALUATION

Before implementing a training program, you need to note specific information to ensure an appropriate regimen. Age and sex are important factors. Most important is medical history; note any chronic health conditions such as asthma or diabetes, musculoskeletal deficiencies and irregularities, or surgical procedures performed. List and describe physical strengths and weaknesses. Without awareness of these conditions, abilities, and weaknesses, it's not possible to design a training program.

Also take into consideration history of fitness training and knowledge of specific exercises. Goals (both the coach's and the athlete's) in basketball are a vital factor. Without goals, there's no focus to the program. Many methods of evaluation are available. Select one that is proven reliable as well as comfortable to implement.

ATHLETE PREPARATION

Unfortunately, many young athletes today are less physically active than young athletes of the past. Often, they disregard the opportunities for their bodies, specifically the neuromuscular system, to adapt to and develop from the natural physical stresses that occur during childhood. If walking, running, bicycle riding, tree climbing, and playing schoolyard games are replaced with carpooling and playing video games, are kids less physically prepared when training and competitions are initiated? Are today's kids prepared to do the exercises they will perform over a prolonged period without breaking down? Will they be able to avoid injury?

A classic question you might hear from a coach or a peer regarding the initiation of a weight training program is "How much can you bench press?" instead of

"How did you prepare to train?" You must establish and practice the fundamentals before advancing to the high-level skills required during competition. The same can be said of weight training. You must become familiar with basic weight training skills and exercise techniques before attempting to lift heavy weights. Depending on present physical condition and training history, it may be necessary to incorporate a period of preparation for weight training before participating in the formal training program. A preparation period will ensure achievement of the necessary physical qualities of soft tissue flexibility; joint mobility; and strength and stability of muscles, tendons, and joints. This period also will enhance overall physical conditioning and work capacity.

A preparation period for weight training does not occur as often as assumed. Yet this is very simply achieved in a fairly short time. Training methods such as Javorek's exercise complexes, which are basic regimens made popular by strength and conditioning coach Istvan "Steve" Javorek, are effective. (*Javorek Complex Conditioning, Second Edition,* 2013.)

PROGRAM PREPARATION

If you are a coach, you must develop proficiency in writing training programs for your athletes. Training programs should be individualized to account for factors such as medical history, sex, biological and training age (experience), the sport, and the position played. The goal of the weight training program is to appropriately organize the application of high stress (weight intensity) in the exercises performed for adaptation of the body to take place. These training exercises are repeatedly performed over time. A properly applied design not only will produce the desired results, but will also prevent excessive fatigue that can result in injury.

Exercise Selection

Many training exercises are available for basketball players. The specific exercises should be based on needs and goals.

Primary exercises are those that often are performed in the standing position; they require balance, coordination, timing, and the contribution of various muscle groups of multiple joints to work in harmony. These primary exercises also allow for heavier weights when appropriate for gains in strength and power.

Assistance exercises require an action that emphasizes a single joint or the execution of an isolated exercise. Examples are leg extension, leg curl, biceps curl, and triceps extension. Although assistance exercises do have their role in training, this book focuses on the primary exercises because these are of greater value for optimal transfer to basketball. Primary multijoint exercises should be the foundation of the training program; assistance (joint isolation) exercises, if deemed necessary, should be considered the fine tuning.

Order of Performance

In the daily order of exercise performance, it is important to perform high-speed power exercises such as the power clean before heavy strength exercises such as the back squat. High-velocity movements are more stressful to the neuromuscular system than slower-velocity strength movements; therefore, you should not attempt high-velocity exercises when fatigued. For example, you likely would demonstrate a higher vertical jump (power activity) after an appropriate warm-up than you would after becoming fatigued from a two- to three-hour basketball practice. However, an effective two- to three-hour basketball practice can still occur after the vertical jump.

If incorporating assistance exercises in the program, perform these exercises at the conclusion of all primary exercises.

Repetitions per Set

The number of repetitions performed in each exercise set varies depending on the needs of the athlete and the type of exercise performed. Although muscle strength and size (hypertrophy) go hand in hand, different set repetitions reflect an emphasis on muscle strength rather than muscle size. The repetitions performed per set for a strength exercise are summarized here:

10 repetitions per set: Gains in physical strength with an emphasis on muscle hypertrophy.

5 or 6 repetitions per set: Greater physical strength gains than with 10 repetitions per set with less emphasis on muscle hypertrophy, although there is still very good development of muscle hypertrophy.

1 to 3 repetitions per set: Greatest gains in physical strength with the least amount of muscle hypertrophy.

For power or high-speed barbell or dumbbell exercises, limit the repetitions per exercise set to 1 to 5. Performing higher repetitions will result in excessive fatigue, limiting both the force output and technique. Poor exercise technique while lifting a weighted barbell, dumbbell, or kettlebell will increase the risk of injury.

As a general rule, when the number of repetitions in a set decreases, the weight to be lifted should increase.

Total Repetitions for a Specific Exercise

The total number of repetitions performed (the total repetition sum of all exercise sets) during a specific exercise is also a consideration in program design. For strength exercises such as the squat and the bench press, the total number of repetitions should not exceed 35, plus or minus 3. For the higher-velocity power exercises, the total number of repetitions should not exceed 25, plus or minus 3, or excessive body fatigue may result.

The guidelines for repetitions per set and the total number of repetitions for a specific exercise will aid in developing the program for each day.

Workout Days per Week

Once you are prepared for an off-season workout program that may be 6, 8, or 12 weeks long (if not longer), the weight training program usually is designed for three or four days per week. These workout days are planned with the goals of enhancing athletic performance while avoiding overtraining (inducing excessive fatigue) as the training program progresses over the prescribed time. This chapter describes a three-day-per-week training program because this type of program is simple to follow yet very effective.

The three-day-a-week program occurs on Mondays, Wednesdays, and Fridays. Each workout day is assigned as a heavy day, a medium day, or a light day. Monday usually is considered the heavy day because it is assumed that you are well rested from the weekend in preparation for the intense Monday workout. During the heavy day, you perform the assigned exercises while lifting the heaviest weights with the highest total volume of repetitions.

Wednesday is the light exercise day. You may perform the same exercises as on Monday or incorporate some different exercises. The weight for each set and total volume of work (repetitions) decreases by 20 to 30 percent from the Monday workout.

Friday is the medium workout day. This day includes all of the same exercises performed during the heavy Monday workout. However, this medium day reduces both the weight of each set and the total volume (repetitions) by 15 to 20 percent, depending on exercise performance, from the heavy workout on Monday.

Variability is key. You must work hard to make the physical gains desired during the workout. However, you must recover from the heavy day to prepare for the next week's heavy workout. The ability to recover from a stressful exercise bout is also the reason a baseball pitcher not only has a pitch count but also rests approximately four days between game-day starts. The pitcher must allow his body to fully recover so that he can pitch optimally during his next performance.

Since Monday is the heavy day, you lift heavy weight, an ideal stimulus for enhancing strength and power. The following light workout on Wednesday allows for recovery from the heavy Monday workout. The medium day on Friday maintains the gains made during the heavy Monday workout but does not excessively stress the body to ensure that the following Monday is another successful heavy workout. The Monday–Wednesday–Friday workouts are programmed with this philosophy:

- Monday: The heavy workout day provides optimal gains in physical qualities.
- Wednesday: The light workout day allows for recovery from the heavy Monday workout.
- Friday: The medium workout day maintains the gains in physical qualities made on the heavy day without causing excessive fatigue in preparation for the next heavy workout day.

Consider the back squat (figure 10.1), which may be programmed as follows:

- Monday: Heaviest weight for back squat is 300 pounds. Total repetitions performed for all exercise sets are 35.
- Wednesday: Heaviest weight lifted is 225 pounds (25 percent reduction in weight from Monday). Total repetitions performed are 25 (25 percent reduction in repetitions from Monday).
- Friday: Heaviest weight lifted is 255 pounds (15 percent reduction in weight from Monday). Total repetitions performed are 30 (15 percent reduction in repetitions from Monday).

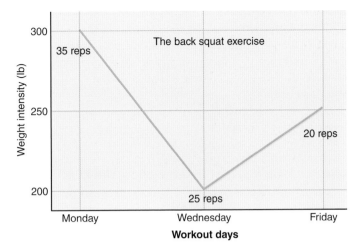

Figure 10.1   Workout week using the back squat as an example.

Strength, Then Power

Both strength and power exercises may be performed simultaneously during the same training period; however, only one physical quality should be emphasized during this training period. For instance, an athlete who is training for a marathon could not simultaneously train for a weightlifting competition. The marathon runner may weight train to help running performance, but the emphasis of marathon training is accumulated distance in one bout, not lifting weights.

The same may be said of strength and power. Strength is the foundation for power. You need to establish adequate strength to generate optimal levels of force before attempting to produce these same forces at higher velocities. If you are not strong enough to generate optimal levels of force, how is it possible for you to apply these absent levels of force at higher velocities? Higher-velocity movements are also stressful to the body. A foundation of strength will enhance output and additional soft tissue and ligament structures and joint integrity, assisting in the prevention of injuries.

Once you are prepared to participate in a training program, the first four weeks of weight training should emphasize strength, which will also induce muscle hypertrophy. At this time you may also introduce power exercises such as Olympic lifts, but the emphasis should be on the technical aspect of performing these higher-speed exercises correctly. At the end of the initial four weeks of strength training, continue with the strength exercises, but the emphasis shifts to the development of power exercises during the next four-week training period.

Designing superior programs, as with any other skill, is established through repetitive practice. The guidelines in this chapter will help in the development of effective training programs.

BIBLIOGRAPHY

Chaouachi, A., M. Brughelli, K. Chamari, G.T. Levin, N. Ben Abdelkrim, L. Laurencelle, and C. Castagna. 2009. Lower limb maximal dynamic strength and agility determinants in elite basketball players. *Journal of Strength and Conditioning Research,* 23(5): 1570-1577.

Chen, S.K., P.T. Simonian, T.L. Wickiewicz, J.C. Otis, and R.F. Warren. 1999. Radiographic evaluation of glenohumeral kinematics: A muscle fatigue model. *Journal of Shoulder and Elbow Surgery*, 8(1): 49-52.

Duncan, R.L., and C.H. Turner. 1995. Mechanotransduction and the functional response of bone to mechanical strain. *Calcified Tissue International,* 57(5): 344-358.

Inman, V.T., J.B. Saunders, and L.C. Abbott. 1944. Observations of the function of the shoulder joint. *Journal of Bone and Joint Surgery*, 26: 1.

Javorek, I. 2013. *Complex conditioning* (2nd ed).

Moseley Jr., J.B., F.W. Jobe, M. Pink, J. Perry, and J. Tibone. 1992. EMG analysis of the scapular muscles during a shoulder rehabilitation program. *American Journal of Sports Medicine*, 20(2): 128-134.

Myer, G.D., D.A. Chu, J.L. Brent, and T.E. Hewett. 2008. Trunk and hip control neuromuscular training for the prevention of knee joint injury. *Clinical Sports Medicine,* 27: 425-448.

Myer, G.D., K.R. Ford, and T.E. Hewett. 2004. Rationale and clinical techniques for anterior cruciate ligament injury prevention among female athletes. *Journal of Athletic Training,* 39(4): 352-364.

Myer, G.D., K.R. Ford, and T.E. Hewett. 2008. Tuck jump assessment for reducing anterior cruciate ligament injury risk. *Athletic Therapy Today,* 13(5): 39-44.

Prodromos, C.C., Y. Han, J. Rogowski, B. Joyce, and K. Shi. 2007. A meta-analysis of the incidence of anterior cruciate ligament tears as a function of gender, sport, and a knee injury-reduction regimen. *Arthroscopy,* 23(12): 1320-1325.

Reeves, N., C. Maganaris, G. Ferretti, and M. Narici. 2005. Influence of 90-day simulated microgravity on human tendon mechanical properties and the effect of resistive countermeasures. *Journal of Applied Physiology,* 98(6): 2278-2286.

Selye, H. 1956. *The Stress of Life.* New York: McGraw-Hill.

Turner, A.N., and I. Jeffreys. 2010. The stretch-shortening cycle: Proposed mechanisms and methods for enhancement. *Strength and Conditioning Journal,* 32(4): 87-99.

Warner, J.J., L.J. Micheli, L.E. Arslanian, J. Kennedy, and R. Kennedy. 1992. Scapulothoracic motion in normal shoulders and shoulders with glenohumeral instability and impingement syndrome. A study using Moiré topographic analysis. *Clinical Orthopaedics and Related Research,* 285: 191-199.

Yin, N.H., W.S. Chen, Y.T. Wu, T.T. Shih, C. Rolf, and H.K. Wang. 2014. Increased patellar tendon microcirculation and reduction of tendon stiffness following knee extension eccentric exercises. *Journal of Orthopaedic and Sports Physical Therapy,* 44(4): 304-312.

EXERCISE FINDER

LEGS: WHERE THE GAME STARTS

LOWER BACK AND CORE: THE CENTER OF STABILITY

UPPER-BODY STRENGTH AND POWER: PULLING EXERCISES

UPPER-BODY STRENGTH AND POWER: PUSHING EXERCISES

EXPLOSIVE WEIGHT TRAINING FOR PLAYING ABOVE THE RIM

PLYOMETRICS FOR A QUICKER FIRST STEP AND GAME REACTION

REHABILITATION FOR OPTIMAL RETURN TO PLAY

INJURY PREVENTION FOR AVOIDING THE BENCH

ABOUT THE AUTHORS

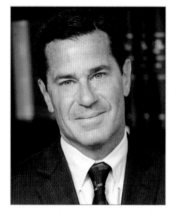 **Dr. Brian Cole**, **M.D., M.B.A**. is a professor in the department of orthopedics with a conjoint appointment in the department of anatomy and cell biology at Rush University Medical Center in Chicago, Illinois. In 2011, he was appointed as chairman of surgery at Rush Oak Park Hospital. He is the section head of the Cartilage Research and Restoration Center at Rush University Medical Center, a multidisciplinary program specializing in the treatment of arthritis in young active patients. He also serves as the head of the orthopedic master's program and trains residents and fellows in sports medicine and research. He lectures nationally and internationally, and through his basic science and clinical research has developed several innovative techniques for the treatment of shoulder, elbow, and knee conditions. He has published more than 1,000 articles and has published five widely read textbooks in orthopedics.

Dr. Cole was chosen as one of the best doctors in America each year since 2004 and as a top doctor in the Chicago metro area each year since 2003. In 2006, he was featured as "Chicago's Top Doctor" and placed on the cover of *Chicago Magazine*. In 2009, Dr. Cole was selected as the NBA Team Physician of the Year. In 2013, *Orthopedics This Week* published that "Dr. Cole was chosen as one of the top 19 sports medicine specialists in the U.S. by his peers." He is the team physician for the Chicago Bulls NBA team, co-team physician for the Chicago White Sox Major League Baseball team and DePaul University in Chicago.

Dr. Brian J. Cole is a member of Midwest Orthopaedics at Rush, the regional leader in comprehensive orthopedic services. He was the recipient of the American Physical Therapy Association Sports Physical Section's 2015 Lynn Wallace Clinical Educator Award.

Rob Panariello, **MS, PT, ATC, CSCS** is a graduate of Ithaca College with a B.S. in both physical therapy and physical education and athletic training. He also holds a master's degree in exercise physiology from Queens College. He is a licensed physical therapist, NATA certified athletic trainer and NSCA certified strength and conditioning specialist. Rob has more than 30 years in the field of athletic training sports rehabilitation and athletic performance.

Rob has studied the science of strength and conditioning in the former East Germany, Soviet Union, and Bulgaria. His experience includes 10 years (1986 – 1995) as the head strength and conditioning coach at St. John's University, the World League of American Football's New York and New Jersey Knights (1991), and the WUSA New York Power Women's Professional Soccer League, (2001-2002). He serves as a consultant to many NFL, NBA, and university teams and strength coaches.

He is nationally renowned in the field of sports medicine, rehabilitation, and strength and conditioning. Rob lectures nationally on these topics and has over 60 peer reviewed publications. Rob received the prestigious National Strength and Conditioning Association President's Award in 1998 and is in the USA Strength and Conditioning Coaches Hall of Fame.